The Gospel

The New Testament translation in this book is wholly from *The Source: With Extensive Notes on Greek Word Meaning*. Translation and Notes by Dr A. Nyland.

dranyland.blogspot.com

Cover: Oxyrhynchus (specifically *Oxyrhynchon polis*) means "City of the Sharp-nosed Fish." The Greek papyrus fragments of The Gospel of Thomas are from Oxyrhynchus.

Contents.

Chapter 1. Glossary.

Metonymy. The substitution of a word describing the nature or significance of an object instead of the object itself. Example: "Here come the suits!" ("Suits" here is metonymy for "business people.")

Semantic range.

The semantic range means all the meanings of a word. A word in one language may have (for example) three different meanings, but only have one of these meanings in another language. Not everything translates across. In the English language, the word "port" can mean an alcoholic drink, the left side of a ship, a piece of baggage, or a place to dock ships. The Greek word for a fortified wine does not however also mean the left side of a ship. In the English language, the word "bear" can mean to put up with someone or something, to carry an item, or a large dangerous animal with big teeth. The Coptic word for a dangerous animal does not include the meaning of carrying an item. The Hebrew word "Seraph" (plural: Seraphim) can mean a fiery snake or an angelic being. However, the English word "snake" cannot mean an angelic being. The English word "taste" is used in the context of food and is not the same word as "experience," but many ancient languages have just the one word with both meanings. It is a translation error to translate the word as "experience" in the context of food, or to translate it as "taste" in the context of experiencing something.

Transliteration.

To "transliterate" (noun, "transliteration") means to put the Coptic or Greek letters into English letters. The original has Coptic or Greek letters which are not like English letters, just as Chinese is not written in letters of the English alphabet. As an example, the transliteration (putting ancient Greek letters of the alphabet into English letters of the alphabet) of a certain Greek word is *anoetos*. The translation is "loss of senses."

Chapter 2. Translator's Note: Let the Buyer Beware.

This book serves as an introduction to The Gospel of Thomas. I have not made theological notes, and if you are interested further, I recommend books by scholars such as Köster or Layton, and advise avoiding rehashed public domain translations. As a translator who has spent many years of postgraduate research on ancient languages and spent time on Faculty at a well-regarded university, I am continually frustrated by the profusion of public domains on the market produced by people with zero knowledge who remarket old out of date public domain translations.

To make matters worse, reader-reviewers often review the actual source text rather than the translation or version, not realizing that there is a crucial difference.

Public domain translations are those out of copyright. Generally speaking, all books published in the United States before 1923 are in the public domain. Shakespeare and the King James Version Bible, for example, are in the public domain.

Many people who know no language other than English find a free public domain translation and publish it, and flood the market with these books. The buyer is not aware of this, as the very same pre-1923 public domain book will appear under twenty or so different covers. Sad to say, the publishing of these public domain versions has at times been pushed as a money making scheme or a get-rich-quick scheme.

Worse still, there are some people who get such public domain translations and alter them slightly, then pretend these are their own translations. The commentary on such books is procured from the internet and also usually is a barely disguised rewording of the commentary (errors and all) on the public domain translation, and is invariably full of serious and most basic errors. Such people, as they know no language other than English and certainly do not know a word of an ancient language, do not even have a grasp of the technical language of translation at even the most basic level, yet the public at large is fooled.

A further problem with public domain translations is that knowledge of word meaning in language has improved vastly in recent times. To take a New Testament example, Matthew 11:12 caused problems for translators and puzzled readers for centuries. Only in recent times was it discovered that the word *bia* refers to illegal forcible acquisition, and is a technical legal term referring to the delict of hindering an owner or lawful possessor of their enjoyment of immovable property. From the papyri, there is now firm evidence to show that both *bia* and *harpage*, together with their cognates, were used in legal terminology with reference to forcible acquisition. We now know the scripture has nothing to do with heaven suffering violence or forcefully advancing. The actual translation is, "From the time of John the Baptizer until now, Heaven's Realm is being used or even robbed by people who have no legal right to it. This stops those who do have a legal right to it from enjoying their own property."

Chapter 3. The Greek Version and the Coptic Version of The Gospel of Thomas.

The Greek fragments of *The Gospel of Thomas* (*GTh*) are from Oxyrhynchus. Oxyrhynchus rose to prominence under Egypt's Hellenistic and Roman rulers and at that time was a highly prosperous regional capital, one of the largest cities in Egypt.[1] Oxyrhynchus was 100 miles (160 km) south west of Memphis and 186 miles (300 km) south of Alexandria.

Oxyrhynchus is of vital importance today because its rubbish dumps were intact until the late nineteenth century. They have yielded vast and crucial pieces of papyri, preserved for centuries under the ideal conditions of profound dryness.

In the late 1880s and again in the mid 1970s, large amounts of papyri were discovered. These impacted our knowledge of word meaning in the New Testament alone to such a degree that New Testament scholars labeled the finds "sensational" and "dramatic." The papyri were written at the time of the New Testament, and touched upon all aspects of life, comprising everyday private letters from ordinary people, contracts of marriage and divorce, tax papers, official decrees, birth and death notices, and business documents. Large numbers of previously uncommon words found in the New Testament now appeared commonly in everyday documents as well as on inscriptions. Many mysteries of word meaning were thus solved.

In 1897, two archaeologists, Grenfell and Hunt, began excavating Oxyrhynchus. Papyrology in general has revolutionised our knowledge of word meaning. Several thousand Greek inscriptions and papyri were published for the first time, or reissued, in 1976. In that year alone, fifteen volumes of new papyri were published. Light was thrown on a large number of words previously unattested. Finds are ongoing: several thousand new inscriptions come to light each year. In the last two decades, four thousand inscriptions have been found at Ephesus alone. Laypersons are unaware of the main body of scholarship as it is tucked away in technical journals.

In 1897 and 1903 three ancient fragments from Greek versions of The Gospel of Thomas were discovered at Oxyrhynchus.

The three Oxyrhynchus fragments preserve 20 of the 114 Sayings (or, in Greek, *logion*) found in the complete Coptic version of The Gospel of Thomas: P.Oxy 1 contains Sayings (*logion*) 26, 27, 28, 29, 30, 31, 77. P.Oxy 654 contains Sayings 1, 2, 3, 4, 5, 6, 7. P.Oxy 655 contains Sayings 36, 37, 38, 39, 40.

These three papyrus fragments have been dated to 130 - 250 CE.

The Nag Hammadi discovery of 1945 unearthed a complete version of *The Gospel of Thomas* in Coptic. This discovery made it possible to identify the Oxyrhunchus texts as fragments of a Greek edition of *The Gospel of Thomas*. While there is close correlation between the two versions, there are also notable differences.

Cameron states that the differences between the Greek fragments and the Coptic text are best explained as variants resulting from the circulation of more than one Greek edition of The Gospel of Thomas in antiquity and cites evidence for the frequent copying of The Gospel of Thomas in the third century CE.[2]

The fragments themselves are not of the same manuscript, but the fragmentary state of the papyri makes it impossible to determine whether any of the manuscripts were copied from one another, or whether they are based on a single source.[3] It is clear that *The Gospel of Thomas* was edited over time. It is also clear that the extant Gospel of Thomas was not the first Coptic transcription made from the Greek.[4] Scholars consider the text of *The Gospel of Thomas* unsound. In those times, scribes commonly added words and phrases, even sections, to the original text.

Note. Some say the Gospel of Thomas is not a "gospel," but "gospel" is simply a Middle English word meaning "Good News" which is the actual term used in the original languages. The word "sayings" (*logion* in ancient Greek) can also apply to a "gospel." Eusebius also quotes Papias as saying, "Matthew compiled the sayings in the Hebrew language, but everyone translated them as they were able".[5] Papias' (c. 130 CE) words appear in a later Latin translation, Against Heresies, Ante-Nicene Fathers, 3.1.1.[6]

Chapter 4. The Dating of The Gospel of Thomas.

The Greek fragments of *The Gospel of Thomas* have been dated to 130 - 250 CE, and the Coptic version is dated to the fourth century.

Scholar Stevan Davies puts forward the argument that *The Gospel of Thomas* may predate our extant versions of the canonical gospels.[7] Let us look at the dating of these.

Matthew frequently speaks against the sect of the Sadducees, which was wiped out in the war with the Romans in 66-70 CE. Likewise, the temple tax mentioned in 17:24-27 did not continue after the temple was destroyed. This effectively places Matthew's work prior to this date. The evidence suggests that Luke and Matthew did not know of each other's work, thus dating both works around the same time as each other. Luke is dated c. 62 CE.[8] The consensus of opinion places Matthew's authorship to the mid 60s CE.

Eusebius quotes Irenaeus c. 170 CE as saying, "Matthew published the Gospel in writing also, among the Hebrews in their own language, while Peter and Paul in Rome were preaching the Gospel and founding the church."[9] Peter and Paul were first in Rome together in the early 60s.[10] There is doubt as to whether the "sayings" are those we know as the Gospel of Matthew. Eusebius quotes of Clement of Rome (c. 101 CE) as saying that the first of the four gospels which are unquestionable was Matthew, "who was once a Tax Profiteer but later an apostle." Clement, writing from Rome to Corinth c. 96 CE, refers to Matthew.[11] Matthew is quoted as early as c. 110 CE by Ignatius[12] and by Polycarp's Letter to the Philippians.[13]

The general academic opinion is that Mark was written before Luke (late 50s to 60s CE) and Romans (c. CE 57) and was used as source material for the other gospels. However, this has been variously disputed. L. Wells[14] makes a further case for the priority of Mark based on his healing language and accounts of healing.

Some suggest that Mark wrote his Gospel in Palestine by the late 40s, while others suggest that Mark wrote the Gospel in Rome in the early to mid 50s. Papias and Clement of Alexandria state (although Irenaeus does not) that Mark wrote his Gospel in connection with Peter while the latter was still living. Papias said,

"Mark became Peter's interpreter and wrote accurately everything that he remembered, certainly not in the order of the things said and done by the Lord. For he had not heard the Lord, nor had he followed him, but later on, as I said, followed Peter, who used to teach as necessity demanded, but not making an arrangement of sayings by the Lord, so that Mark did nothing wrong in writing down single points as he remembered them. He was most careful to leave nothing out of what he had heard and to make no false statement in his writings."[15]

Note that Mark was closely associated with Peter (who, according to Eusebius, died in 64 CE) in Jerusalem in the 40s (Acts 12:12) and the 60s (1 Pet. 5:13). However, there is a possibility that the young man in 14:51-52 was Mark himself. A literary device of the times was for the author to identify themselves by means of a token. The author would identify themselves by allusion.

Luke was recognized as the author of this Gospel from the early second century. Eusebius, Irenaeus, Tertullian, Clement of Alexandria, Origen, Jerome, the Muratorian Canon, and the anti-Marcionite Prologue to Luke all attest to authorship by Luke both of the Gospel and of Acts. The Muratorian Canon[16] states, "The third Gospel book according to Luke. Luke, this physician, after the Anointed One's ascension, since Paul had taken him as an expert in the way, composed it in his own name according to his own thinking. Yet he did he not see the Lord in the flesh."[17]

The date is not known precisely: it was after the late 50s, and before the end of the 60s. The book of Acts ends before Paul's trial was over, suggesting that it was written prior to 62/3 CE. It is clear that Luke-Acts is a two volume work[18] and that Luke was written prior to Acts. Matthew and Luke have independently used Mark. The evidence suggests that Matthew and Luke were unaware of each other's work, and thus should be dated around the same time as each other. Matthew was written prior to the war with the Romans in 66-70 CE, and Acts covers events up to 63 CE. 62 CE seems to be the most likely date for the writing of Luke's Gospel.

John, the son of Zebedee (and the brother of James), knew Jesus very well. He had been one of the Twelve disciples, and had gone with Peter and James to the Jews after the Jerusalem meeting c. 47 CE. John's Gospel is clearly pre-war and written before 66 CE. John states that the pool has (not had) 5 porticoes, and describes the temple as still standing. Both were not standing after the catastrophic war of 66-70 CE between the Jews and the Romans in Palestine. In the war the temple was destroyed as were many parts of Jerusalem. The reference to Peter's prophesied manner of death in John 21:19 possibly suggests that John's Gospel was written after 64 CE, the date of Peter's death in the Neronian persecution.

It is often said that P^{52} (John 18: 31-33, 37-38) is the earliest fragment of any New Testament book found to date, having been assigned to the first half of the second century by its editor, C.H. Roberts. However, it is subject to ongoing scrutiny and has been dated to 170 CE by A. Schmidt.[19] In the 1983, P^{90} was published: P.Oxy. L 3523 (Oxyrhynchos, II?) The text of P^{90} overlaps with that of P^{52}, as with that of P^{66} and P^{60}. P^{90} is dated to the first half of the second century by its editor, T.C. Skeat, and is generally considered to be close to date to P^{52}.[20]

The authorship of John has been widely undisputed from the beginning of the second century. The church fathers from Irenaeus onwards do not question John's authorship.[21] Clement of Alexandria wrote, "Last of all John, perceiving that the external facts had been set forth in the Gospels, at the insistence of his disciples and with the inspiration of the Spirit, composed a spiritual Gospel."[22] As for the title, early papyri and 5th c. papyri have "The Gospel According to John", while later manuscripts attest to the title, "The Sacred Gospel According to John" Another title, "According to John" is also attested.

The traditional site for the writing of John's Gospel is Ephesos. Irenaeus (A.H. 3.1.1. c. 180 CE) says that John, "the Lord's disciple", wrote his Gospel at Ephesos, after the writing of the other gospels. Justin Martyr (Dialogue with Trypho 81.4) speaks of John as having lived previously at Ephesos. John Martyr was in Ephesos c. 135 CE. Eusebius (H.E. 4.18.6-8) also records that John the Apostle lived at Ephesos. The Acts of John, written by Leucius Charinus c. 150 CE, speaks of the ministry of "John the Apostle" at Ephesos. Eusebius (H.E. 5.24.3) notes that Polycrates, bishop of Ephesos, writing to Pope Victor of Rome c. 190 CE, states that "John the Apostle" was buried at Ephesos.

Chapter 5. Thomas's Name.

Some internet sites say that Thomas ("twin") was also named Didymus ("twin"). However, Thomas was the Hebrew word for "twin" and Didymus (Greek for 'twin") was simply the Greek translation name.

Some also wrongly state that Jude carries the sense "Twin" in Aramaic. The Greek name Ioudas is often rendered by the English name "Judas" or "Jude." It was a very common name of the time. The Hebrew name Judah means "one who is praised." It is often rendered by the English name "Judas" or "Jude."

Double names are attested in the papyri and inscriptions[23] in specifically Jewish papyri and inscriptions[24] and in Josephus.[25] There are several types of double names mentioned in the New Testament.

(1) The Jewish name plus name which was originally patronymic but developed into a proper name (Joseph + Barsabbas; Judas + Barsabbas; Joseph + Barnabas; Elymas + Barjesus).

(2) Jewish name plus place of origin used as a name (Mary +Magdalene; Judas + Iscariot).

(3) Jewish name (graecised) plus descriptive name or nickname (Simon + zealot, Simeon + Canaanite).

(4) Jewish name plus Roman name (Saul + Paul, John + Mark, Jesus + Justus, Simon + Niger, Joseph + Justus).

(5) Jewish names with Greek/Roman substitute names: Symeon/Simon, Silas/Silvanus. Priska is the diminutive substitute of the Roman name Priscilla.

(6) Jewish names with Greek translation names: Cephas/Peter; Thomas/Didymos, Tabitha/Dorcas.

(7) Jewish name + title (for example, Christos.)[26] Early Christians frequently took on names of pagan gods (see Eusebius, de martyribus Palaestinae 11.8) (and note Epaphroditus in the New Testament), but after the first couple of centuries abandoned such names in favor of names of prophets. Christians commonly took on names of the prophets, but the practice did not continue, that is, New Testament names were not generally taken on.[27] Horsley comments that many names had meanings relevant to the bearer: e.g. Oidipous,

Elektra, Onesimus, Chrestus, Thratta, Phryx, Demosthenes, Themistokles, and that the significance of the meaning of names did appear to diminish with time.[28]

Chapter 6. The Gospel of Thomas.

Prologue and 1. The Gospel of Thomas.

Coptic
Prologue and 1) These are the secret sayings which the living Jesus spoke and which Didymos Judas Thomas wrote down. He said, "Whoever understands these sayings will not experience death."

Greek
Prologue and 1) These are the secret sayings which were spoken by Jesus the Living One, and which Judas called Thomas wrote down. He said to them, "Whoever hears these words will never experience death."

New Testament.
John 8:51.

Let me emphasize this, anyone who holds on firmly to my Word will not experience death, ever!"

Notes.
"Experience." Some wrongly translate this as "taste." The semantic range includes both "experience" and "taste" and the word should be translated as "taste" only when used in the context of foods.

2. Gospel of Thomas.
Coptic
2) Jesus said, "Let the one who seeks continue seeking until they find what they are looking for. When they find it, they will become troubled. When they become troubled, they will be amazed, and they will rule over the All."

Greek
2) [Jesus said]: "Let the one who seeks not cease until they find, and when they find they will be amazed; being amazed they will reign, and reigning they will rest."

Notes.

In the last 200 years or so people have traditionally used the English word "he" as the third person generic singular, but it is now being replaced by "they." "They" as the third person generic singular is a linguistic singular. In fact, Jane Austen, C.S. Lewis, and Shakespeare among others, commonly used the pronoun "they" instead of "he."

3. Gospel of Thomas.
Coptic

3)   Jesus said, "If those who lead you say, 'Look, the Realm is in the sky,' then the birds of the sky will precede you. If they say to you, 'It is in the sea,' then the fish will precede you. Rather, the Realm is inside of you and outside of you. When you come to know yourselves, then you will become known, and you will realize that it is you who are the children of the living Father. But if you will not know yourselves, you live in poverty and it is you yourselves who are that poverty."

Greek

3)   Jesus said, "If those pulling you say, 'Look! The Realm is in the sky,' then the birds of the sky will precede you, or if they say to you, 'It is under the earth,' then the fish of the sea will precede you. The Realm of God is inside you and outside you. Those who know themselves will find it; and when you know yourselves, you will know that you are children of the living Father. But if you will not know yourselves, you are in poverty and you are the poverty."

New Testament.
Luke 17:20 - 21.

Once Jesus was asked by the Pharisees when God's Realm would come. Jesus said, "God's Realm won't come just because you're watching for it, and neither can people say, 'Here it is!' or 'There it is', because God's Realm is actually within you!"

Notes.

The phrase often translated "Kingdom of God" is correctly the Realm where God's way of doing things happens, where God's will is exercised as God wishes it.

4. Gospel of Thomas.
Coptic

4) Jesus said, "An old man will not hesitate to ask a small child seven days old about the place of life, and he will live. For many who are first will become last, and they will become one and the same."

Greek

4) Jesus said: "An aged person will not hesitate to ask a child seven days old about their place in life and they will live. For many that are first will be last, and many of the last will be first, and they will become one."

New Testament.
Mark 9:35-37.

Jesus sat down, called over the Twelve, and said, "If anyone wants to be first, that person will be the last of all and everyone's servant." He picked up a little child and stood the child in front of them. He hugged the child and said, "The person who welcomes one of these little children in my name welcomes me, and the person who welcomes me doesn't actually welcome me, but actually welcomes the One who sent me."

5. Gospel of Thomas.
Coptic

5) Jesus said, "Recognize what is in your sight, and then that which is hidden from you will become clear to you. For there is nothing hidden which will not come to light."

Greek

5) Jesus said, "Recognize what is in front of your face, and what has been is hidden from you will be revealed to you. There is nothing hidden that will not be made clear, and nothing buried that will not be raised."

New Testament.
Luke 8:17.

All hidden things will be plainly shown; all secret things will come out into the open.

Luke 12:2.

Everything that is completely covered will be revealed, and everything that is hidden will come out into the open.

Matthew 10:26. (Some include this verse as a parallel, so I have included it here. However, the context is that Jesus was speaking about the Pharisees, so this passage is not relevant to the context.)

"Don't be afraid of them! Everything will come out into the open."

6. Gospel of Thomas.
Coptic

6) Jesus' disciples asked him, "Do you want us to fast? How should we pray? Should we give charitable donations? What diet are we to observe?"

Jesus said, "Do not tell lies, and do not do what you hate, for all things are plain in the sight of Heaven's sight. There is nothing hidden that will not become visible, and nothing covered that will stay uncovered."

Greek

6) His disciples asked him, "How do you want us to fast? How should we pray? Are we to give charitable donations? What food laws should we follow?"

Jesus said, "Do not lie, and do not do what you hate, because the truth makes everything clear. There is nothing hidden which will not be made clear."

New Testament.
Luke 11:1.

At one point Jesus was praying in a certain place. When he finished, one of his disciples said to him, "Lord, please teach us how to pray, just like John taught his disciples to pray too."

Luke 8:17.

All hidden things will be plainly shown; all secret things will come out into the open.

Luke 12:2.

Everything that is completely covered will be revealed, and everything that is hidden will come out into the open.

Matthew 10:26. (Some include this verse as a parallel, so I have included it here. However, the context is that Jesus was speaking about the Pharisees, so this passage is not relevant to the context.)

"Don't be afraid of them! Everything will come out into the open."

7. Gospel of Thomas.
Coptic

7)   Jesus said, "Blessed is the lion which becomes human when eaten by a human; and cursed is the human whom the lion consumes, and the lion becomes human."

Greek

7) Blessed is...

8. Gospel of Thomas.
Coptic

8)   He said, "The Realm is like a wise fisherman who cast his net into the sea and drew it up from the sea full of small fish. Among them the wise fisherman found a fine large fish. He threw all the small fish back into the sea and chose the large fish without difficulty. If you have ears you had better listen!'"

New Testament.
Matthew 13:9.
"If you have ears you had better listen!"

Mark 4:9.
He added, "If you have ears you had better listen!"

Luke 8:8.
After Jesus said this, he shouted, "If you have ears you had better listen!"

Matthew 13:47-48.

This is a story about Heaven's Realm. It is like a net that was cast into the sea and drew up some of every kind of fish. When it was full, they hauled it to shore and sat down and put the good fish in storage, but threw the bad fish away.

9. Gospel of Thomas.
Coptic

9) Jesus said, "Now the sower went out, took a handful of seeds, and scattered them. Some fell on the road. The birds came and took them. Others fell on the rock, so did not take root in the soil, and did not produce ears. Others fell on thorns which choked the seeds and worms ate them. Others fell on good soil and produced good harvest. It produced sixty per measure and a hundred and twenty per measure."

New Testament.
Matthew 13:3-8.

He told them many things in examples. "A farmer went out to sow seed. While he was sowing, some seed fell on the roadside, and the birds ate it. Some seed fell on shallow soil over gravel. The plants immediately sprang up but when the sun came up, they got scorched and withered away because they didn't have any roots. Some seed fell among thorns which shot up and choked them. Other seed fell on fertile ground and produced a harvest. The harvest produced thirty, sixty, or even a hundred times more than had been sown.

Mark 4:3-8.

"Listen!" he instructed. "A farmer went to sow seed. In the process of sowing the seed, some seed fell along the path, and the birds came and ate it up. Some seed fell on stony ground, the sort of place where there wasn't much soil. It shot straight up, but because the soil didn't have depth, it got scorched when the sun came up, and withered away because there were no roots. Other seed fell around the thorny plants. They grew and choked the seeds, so they didn't produce any grain. Still other individual seeds[29] fell on favorable soil. They grew and ripened and produced a crop – some individual seed multiplied 30 times, some 60 times, and some 100 times!"

Luke 8:5-8.

"The farmer went out to plant his seed. As the farmer was planting the seed, some[30] fell along the road - it was trampled on, and the birds ate it up. But some other seed fell on rocky ground, and when it grew, it withered because it didn't have any moisture. But some other seed fell among thorns, and the thorns grew up with it and choked it. Still other seed fell on good soil. It grew and produced a crop a hundred times more than was planted." After Jesus said this, he shouted, "If you have ears you had better listen!"

10. Gospel of Thomas.
Coptic

10) Jesus said, "I have directed fire upon the world, and look, I am guarding it until it burns!"

New Testament.
Luke 12:49.

I have come to bring fire on the earth, and how I wish it had already started!

11. Gospel of Thomas.
Coptic

11) Jesus said, "This heaven will pass away, and the one above it will pass away. The dead are not alive, and the living will not die. In the days when you consumed what is dead, you made it alive. When you come to live in the light, what will you do? On the day when you were one you became two. But when you become two, what will you do?"

New Testament.

Matthew 24:35.

The sky and the earth will pass away, but my words will by no means pass away.

Note: In Greek, the word for "sky" and "heaven" is the same.

12. Gospel of Thomas.
Coptic
12) The disciples asked Jesus, "We know that you will leave us. Who is to be our leader?"

Jesus answered them, "Wherever you are, you are to go to James the just, for whose sake heaven and earth came into being."

13. Gospel of Thomas.
Coptic
13) Jesus said to his disciples, "Compare me to someone and tell me who I am like."

Simon Peter said to him, "You are like a just angel."

Matthew said to him, "You are like a wise philosopher."

Thomas said to him, "Master, I am completely incapable of saying who you are like."

Jesus said, "I am not your master. Because you have drunk, you have become intoxicated by the bubbling spring which I have measured out."

He withdrew with him and told him three things. When Thomas returned to his companions, they asked him, "What did Jesus say to you?"

Thomas answered, "If I tell you one of the things which he told me, you will pick up stones and throw them at me. A fire will come out of the stones and burn you up."

New Testament.
Mark 8: 27-30.

Jesus and his disciples went off to the villages of Caesarea Philippi. Along the road he asked them, "Who do people think I am?"

They answered, "Some say John the Baptizer, but others say Elijah, still others say one of the Prophets."

"But what about you – who do you think I am?" Jesus asked.

"You're the Anointed One," Peter answered.

Jesus forbade them to tell anyone about him.

14. Gospel of Thomas.
Coptic
14) Jesus said to them, "If you fast, you will cause to harm to yourselves. If you pray, you will be condemned. If you give

charitable donations, you will cause harm to your lives. When you go into any land and walk around in the districts, if they receive you, eat what they set before you, and heal the sick among them. What goes into your mouth will not pollute you - it's what comes out of your mouth that will pollute you."

New Testament.
Luke 10:8-9,
When you go into a city and they welcome you, eat what they put in front of you. Heal the sick there and tell them, 'God's Realm is close to you.'

Matthew 15:11.
It's not what goes into the mouth that pollutes a person, but it's what comes out of the mouth that pollutes a person.

Mark 7:15.
Nothing outside a person can make a person polluted by going into them! Instead, it's what comes out of a person that makes a person polluted!"

15. Gospel of Thomas.
Coptic
15) Jesus said, "When you see one who was not born of woman, prostrate yourselves on your faces and worship him. That one is your Father."

16. Gospel of Thomas.
Coptic
16) Jesus said, "Humans perhaps think it is peace that I have come to cast upon the world. They do not know that I have come to cast dissension on the earth: fire, sword, and war. There will be five in a house: three will be against two, and two against three, the parent against the child, and the child against the parent. And they will stand solitary."

New Testament.
Matthew 10:34-36.
"Don't think that I came to bring peace on the earth! No, I have come with a razor blade, to cut between a person and their parent, a

daughter and her mother, a daughter-in-law and her mother-in-law! Someone's enemies will be those close to them!

Luke 12:51-53.

Do you think I came to bring peace on earth? Not at all, I tell you - not peace, but division. From now on there will be five in one family divided against each other, three against two and two against three. They will be divided - father against son and son against father, mother against daughter and daughter against mother, mother-in-law against daughter-in-law and daughter-in-law against mother-in-law.

17. Gospel of Thomas.
Coptic
17) Jesus said, "I will give you what no eye has seen, what no ear has heard, what no hand has touched and what has never occurred to the human mind."

New Testament.
1 Corinthians 2:9.

The Scriptures say, "Eye has not seen nor ear heard, nor has it occurred to a person, the things which God has prepared for those who love God."[31]

18. Gospel of Thomas.
Coptic
18) The disciples said to Jesus, "Tell us what our end will be."

Jesus said, "Have you then discovered the beginning, that you look for the end? The end will be where the beginning is. Blessed is the one who will take their place in the beginning; they will know the end and will not experience death."

19. Gospel of Thomas.
Coptic
19) Jesus said, "Blessed is the one who came into being before that one came into being. If you become my disciples and listen to my words, these stones will minister to you. There are five trees for you in Paradise[32] which remain undisturbed summer and winter and whose leaves do not fall. Whoever becomes acquainted with them will not experience death."

20. Gospel of Thomas.
Coptic
20) The disciples said to Jesus, "Tell us what the Realm of Heaven is like."

He said to them, "It is like a mustard seed, the smallest of all seeds. But when it falls on tilled soil, it becomes a mighty plant and becomes a shelter for the birds of the sky."

New Testament.
Matthew 13:31-32.

He set another example in front of them: "This is a story about Heaven's Realm. Someone planted a mustard seed in their field. A mustard seed is the smallest of all the seeds – that's for sure! But when it grows it's even larger than vegetables. In fact, it grows into a tree, and even birds roost in its branches!"

Mark 4:30-32.

Jesus continued, "What can we say God's Realm is like, or how will we describe it? It is like a mustard seed, which is the smallest seed that you sow in the ground. And when it is sown, it grows and becomes the biggest of all garden-herbs. It shoots out such large branches that birds can perch in its shade."

Luke 13:18-19.

Then Jesus asked, "What is God's Realm like? What can I compare it with? It is like a mustard seed which a person took and planted in the garden. It grew and turned into a tree, and the birds came and perched in its branches."

21. Gospel of Thomas.
Coptic
21) Mary said to Jesus, "Who are your disciples like?"

He answered her, "They are like children who have settled in a field which is not theirs. When the owners of the field come, they will say, 'Give us our field back.' They will undress in their presence in order to let them have their field back. They will give it back to them. So I say to you, if the owner of a house knows that the thief is coming, he will start his vigil before the thief comes and will not let him into his house or his domain to steal his goods. You are to be on your guard against the world.

"Arm yourselves with great strength, otherwise the robbers could find a way to come to you, and the difficulty which you expect will certainly materialize. Let there be among you a person with understanding. When the grain ripened, he came quickly with his sickle in his hand and reaped it. If you have ears you had better listen!"

New Testament.
Matthew 24:43.

Realize this, that if the owner of the household had known the time of the night the thief would come, they would have kept their wits about them and not allowed their house to be broken into.

Luke 12:39.

But understand this - if the owner of the house had known what time the thief was coming, he wouldn't have let his house be broken in to.

Mark 4:26-29.

"This is a story about God's Realm," Jesus said. "A person throws seed on the ground, sleeps at night and gets up in the day, and the seed sprouts[33] and grows, yet the person doesn't know how. The earth of its own accord grows fruit, first the blade, then the ear of grain, then the full grain. But when the grain ripens, the person immediately sends out the harvesting equipment, because the harvest has arrived."

22. Gospel of Thomas.
Coptic

22) Jesus saw infants being nursed. He said to his disciples, "These infants being nursed are like those who enter the Realm."

They replied, "So then do we enter the Realm like children?"

Jesus said to them, "When you make the two one, and when you make the inside like the outside and the outside like the inside, and the above like the below, and when you make the male and the female one and the same, so that the male is not male and the female is not female; and when you make eyes in the place of an

28

eye, and a hand in place of a hand, and a foot in place of a foot, and a likeness in place of a likeness, then will you enter the Realm."

New Testament.
Matthew 18:3.
He said, "Let me emphasize this, unless you change and become like children, there is no way you will enter Heaven's Realm!

Luke 18:17.
There is absolutely no way that someone who doesn't accept God's Realm like a little child will ever enter it.

Matthew 5:29-30.
If your right eye sets a trap for you, rip it out and throw it away! It's better for one of your body parts to perish, than for your whole body to be thrown into the Garbage Pit Gehenna. **30** And if your right hand sets a trap for you, cut it off and throw it away! It's better for one of your body parts to perish, than for your whole body to be thrown into the Garbage Pit Gehenna.

Mark 9:43-48.
"If your hand sets a trap for you, then cut it off!" he continued. "It's better[34] for you to go into life disabled than to have two hands and to be thrown into the fire of the Garbage Pit Gehenna[35] that can't be put out.[36] If your foot sets a trap for you, cut it off! It's better for you to go into life crippled than to have two feet and be thrown into the Garbage Pit Gehenna.[37] If your eye sets a trap for you, throw it away! It's better for you to enter God's Realm with one eye than to be thrown into the Garbage Pit Gehenna, 'where the maggots don't die and the fire can't be put out.'[38]

23. Gospel of Thomas.
Coptic
23) Jesus said, "I will choose you, one out of a thousand, and two out of ten thousand, and they will stand as one."

24. Gospel of Thomas.[39]
Coptic
24) His disciples said to him, "Show us the place where you are, since it is necessary for us to find it."

He said to them, "If you have ears you had better listen. There is light within a person of light, and it lights up the whole world. If it does not shine, it is darkness."

New Testament.
John 13:36.

Simon Peter asked, "Lord, where are you going?"

Jesus answered, "Where I'm going, you won't be able to follow now, but you will be able to later."

Matthew 6:22-23.

The body's light is generosity.[40] If you are generous, you will be full of light. But if you are greedy,[41] your whole body will be in darkness! And if the light in you is in fact dark, then the darkness in you is huge!

Luke 11:33-36.

"No one lights a portable lamp and hides it somewhere, or puts it under a bucket! Instead they put it on a lamp stand, so it shines light on everyone. Your eye is the lamp of your whole body. When your eyes are generous then your whole body is full of light too. But when they're stingy,[42] your body is full of darkness. So be careful that the light in you is not dark. If your whole body is full of light, and none of it is dark, then it will be completely lit up like when a beam of light shines on you!"

25. Gospel of Thomas.
Coptic
25) Jesus said, "Love your brother/associate like your soul, guard him like the pupil of your eye."

New Testament.
Romans 12:9-11.

Your love[43] for the fellow believers[44] is to be affectionate and warm. Honor one another above yourselves.

Notes.

Adelphoi. Adelphos, singular; *adelphoi*, plural. The Greek word *adelphos* can mean "sibling" (of either gender), a member (male or female) of an association ("fellow believer" in the case of Christians or Jews), a "husband" or "wife" as a term of address between spouses, and in the plural can mean "brothers and sisters" ("siblings"); and "fellow members (of an association)." The Greek word for "sister" is either *adelphos* or, far more commonly, *adelphe*, but for siblings which include females as well as males, the word is *adelphoi*. Thus the plural, *adelphoi*, can mean siblings or members of an association. In English, we say "brothers and sisters", but Greek commonly does not do that. The Greek says *adelphoi*. For example, *P.Oxy* 713 (Oxyrhynchos A.D. 97) states, "My father died leaving me and my *adelphoi* Diodorus and Theis, his heirs, and his property transferred to us." Note that Diodorus is a man's name, and Theis is a woman's name. The word is commonly used in the meaning "fellow believer/s."[45]

26. Gospel of Thomas.
Coptic

26) Jesus said, "You see the beam in your brother's/associate's eye, but you do not see the beam in your own eye. When you remove the beam from your own eye, then you will see clearly to remove the beam from your brother's/associate's eye."

Greek

26) ". . . and then you will see clearly to remove the speck that is in your brother's/fellow believer's/associate's eye."

New Testament.

Matthew 7:3-5.

And why is it that you look at the splinter in your fellow believer's eye, but don't give a thought to the plank of wood in your own eye? How can you say to your fellow believer, 'Let me take out the splinter in your eye,' but there's a plank of wood in your own eye!

Luke 6:41-42.

"Why is it that you look at the splinter in your fellow believer's eye, but don't give a thought to the plank of wood in your own eye?

Why is it that you can say your fellow believer, 'Fellow believer, let me remove that splinter in your eye,' when you don't even take any notice of the plank of wood in your own eye!

27. Gospel of Thomas.
Coptic
27) Jesus said, "If you do not fast from the world, you will not find the Realm. If you do not observe the Sabbath as a Sabbath, you will not see the Father."

Greek
27) Jesus said: "Unless you fast from the world, you will not find the Realm of God, and if you do not keep the Sabbath a Sabbath, you shall not see the Father."

28. Gospel of Thomas.
Coptic
28) Jesus said, "I took my place in the midst of the world, and I appeared to them in the flesh. I found all of them intoxicated; I found none of them thirsty. My soul grieved for the humans, because their minds are blind in their hearts and they do not see. They came into the world empty, and they intend to leave the world empty. But for the moment they are intoxicated. When they shake off their wine, then they will change their minds."[46]

Greek
28) Jesus said: "I stood in the midst of the world, and I appeared to them in the flesh. I found all intoxicated, and I found none of them thirsty. My soul grieved over the human lives, because their minds are blind and they do not see."

29. Gospel of Thomas.[47]
Coptic
29) Jesus said, "If the flesh came into being because of spirit, it is a wonder. But if spirit came into being because of the body, it is a wonder of wonders. Certainly, I am amazed at how this great wealth has made its home in this poverty."

30, 30/77 Gospel of Thomas.
Coptic
30) Jesus said, "Where there are three gods, they are gods. Where there are two or one, I am with him."

Greek
30/77) Jesus said: "Where there are three, they are not without God, and when there is one alone, I say I am with them. Raise the stone, and there you will find me. Split the wood, and there I am."

(Note: This is divided into 30 in the Coptic and 77 in the Coptic.)

New Testament.
Matthew 18:20.

For where two or three people are gathered together in my Name, I am certainly there in their midst.

31. Gospel of Thomas.
Coptic
31) Jesus said, "No prophet is accepted in his own home town. No physician heals those who know him."

Greek
31) Jesus said: "A prophet is not acceptable in his own home town; neither does a physician perform cures for those that know him."

New Testament.

Mark 6:4.

Jesus said to them, "No prophet has honor in their own homeland, among their own relatives, and in their own house."

Luke 4:23-24.

23 Jesus responded, "I am sure[48] you will quote this proverb to me, 'Doctor,[49] heal[50] yourself!' Do the things in your own hometown that we've heard that you did in Capernaum!"

24 "It's a fact that no prophet is accepted in their own hometown," he continued.[51]

John 4:44.

For Jesus himself testified that a prophet has no respect in his own native land.

32. Gospel of Thomas.
Coptic

32) Jesus said, "A city being built on a high mountain and fortified cannot fall, nor can it be hidden."

Greek

32) Jesus said: "A city built and fortified on the top of a high mountain can neither fall nor be hidden."

New Testament.

Matthew 5:14.

You are the light to light up the world. A city on the top of a hill can't be hidden!

33. Gospel of Thomas.
Coptic

33) Jesus said, "Preach from your housetops that which your ears hear. No one lights a lamp and puts it under a bucket, nor do they put it in a hidden place. Instead, they place it on a lamp stand so that everyone who enters and leaves will see its light."

Greek

Jesus said: "What you hear with one ear......

New Testament.

Matthew 10:27.

What I tell you now in the dark, speak in broad daylight! What you hear in private, go public with!

Matthew 5:15.

And who puts a bucket over a light? Instead, they put a light somewhere where it will shine light on everything in the house.

Mark 4:21.

He said to them, "Surely you don't put a lamp under a bucket or under a bed? Shouldn't it be put on a lamp stand?

Luke 8:16.

"No one lights a portable lamp and covers it with a bucket or puts it under a bed. Instead, they put it somewhere where it will shine light on everything, so people who come in can see the light. All hidden things will be plainly shown; all secret things will come out into the open.

Luke 11:33.

No one lights a portable lamp and hides it somewhere, or puts it under a bucket! Instead they put it on a lamp stand, so it shines light on everyone.

34. Gospel of Thomas.
Coptic

34) Jesus said, "If a blind person leads a blind person, they will both fall into a pit."

New Testament.
Matthew 15:14.

You are the light to light up the world. A city on the top of a hill can't be hidden!

Luke 6:39.

He also told them this example: "Can a blind person lead another blind person! Won't they both fall into a ditch!

35. Gospel of Thomas.
Coptic

35) Jesus said, "It is not possible for anyone to enter the house of a strong man and take it by force unless he ties him up. Then he will be able to loot his house."

New Testament.
Matthew 12:29.

How can someone break into a strong person's house and rob it, unless they tie up[52] the strong person first? Then they can take off with the whole lot!

Mark 3:27.

But it isn't possible for someone to go into a strong person's house and plunder their possessions,[53] unless they tie up the strong person first. Then they can make off with[54] the property.[55]

Luke 11:21-22.

"As long as a strong person, fully armed, guards their own house, their possessions are safe. But as soon as someone stronger comes along, attacks and overpowers the strong person, the stronger one takes away the protection on which the strong person relied, and shares out the weapons stripped from the enemy.

36. Gospel of Thomas.
Coptic

36) Jesus said, "Do not worry from morning until evening and from evening until morning about what you will wear."

Greek

36) Jesus said, "Do not worry from dawn to dusk and from dusk to dawn about what food you will eat, or what you will wear. You are far more important than the lilies, which do not card nor spin. What will you wear when you have no clothes? Who would add to your height?[56] It is he who will give you your clothing.

New Testament.
Matthew 6:25.

This is why I tell you this: don't worry about your life, what you're going to eat or what you're going to drink. Don't worry about your body, about what clothes you will wear. Isn't life more important than food? Isn't the body more important than clothing?

Luke 12:22-26.

Then Jesus said to his disciples, "This is why I tell you – don't worry about your life - what you're going to eat - or about your body - what you're going to wear. Life is more important than food, and the body is more important than clothes. Think about the ravens. They don't plant or harvest crops, and they don't have a bank or a barn, and God feeds them. And look how much more valuable you are than birds! Which of you can add any time to your lifespan just by worrying?[57] So since you can't even do this little thing, why do you worry about the rest?

37. Gospel of Thomas.
Coptic
37) His disciples said, "When will you be revealed to us? When will we see you?"

Jesus said, "When you disrobe without being ashamed and take your clothes and place them under your feet like little children and tread on them, then you will see the Living One, and you will not be afraid."

Greek
37) His disciples asked him, "When will you be visible to us? When will we see you?"

He said, "When you strip naked without being ashamed, and take your garments and put them under your feet like little children and tread on them. Then you will see the Living One, and you will not be afraid."

38. Gospel of Thomas.
Coptic
38) Jesus said, "Many times you wanted to hear the words I am saying to you, and you have no one else to hear them from. There will be days when you look for me and will not find me."

39. Gospel of Thomas.
Coptic
39) Jesus said, "The Pharisees and the scribes have taken the keys of Knowledge and hidden them. They themselves have not

entered, nor have they allowed those who wish to enter do so. You, however, are to be as wise as serpents and as innocent as doves."

Greek
Jesus said, "The Pharisees and the scribes took the keys of Knowledge. They hid them. They did not enter, nor did they allow those trying to enter to do so. You, however, are to be as wise as snakes and as innocent as doves."

New Testament.
Luke 11:52.
"Woe to you experts in the Law because you have taken away the key to the door of knowledge. You yourselves didn't go in, and you have stopped people who were trying to enter!"

Matthew 10:16.
I'm sending you out like sheep into a pack of wolves! So have the practical wisdom of serpents and be as uncorrupted as doves.

40. Gospel of Thomas.
Coptic
40) Jesus said, "A grapevine has been planted outside the Father, but as it is unsound, it will be pulled up by the roots and destroyed."

New Testament.
Matthew 15:13.
Jesus replied, "Every plant which my Father of heaven hasn't planted will be uprooted!

41. Gospel of Thomas.
Coptic
41) Jesus said, "Whoever has something in their hand will receive more, and whoever has nothing will be deprived of even the little they have."

New Testament.
Matthew 25:29.

Even more – to overflowing! - will be given to a person who has! But a person who doesn't have – even what they do have will be taken away!

Luke 19:26.

He replied, 'I tell you – to the person who has, more will be given, but to the person who doesn't have, what they do have will be taken away.'

42. Gospel of Thomas.
Coptic
42) Jesus said, "Become passers-by."

43. Gospel of Thomas.
Coptic
43) His disciples said to him, "Who are you, that you should say these things to us?"

Jesus replied, "You do not realize who I am from what I say to you, but you have become like the Jews, for they either love the tree and hate its fruit or love the fruit and hate the tree."

New Testament.
John 8:22-25.

So the Jews said, "Surely he's not going to kill himself! Is that why he says, 'You can't go where I'm going?'"

Jesus said to them, "You people are from below, but I am from above. You are from this world, but I'm not from this world. *24* I told you that you would die while you still have your sins. If you don't believe that I'm the One I claim to be, then you will die while you still have your sins, that's for sure!"

"Who are you?" they asked.

"Exactly what I've been claiming all along!" Jesus answered. "I have many things to say to you and to judge you for, but the One who sent me is truthful. What I've heard from him I'll tell the world."

Matthew 7:16-20.

You will have no trouble recognizing them by the consequences of their actions. Does anyone pick grapes from thorn bushes, or figs from thistles? Nice fruit grows on good trees, but evil fruit grows on rotten trees. Evil fruit can't grow on a good tree, and nice fruit can't grow on a rotten tree. Every tree that doesn't produce nice fruit is cut down and thrown into the fire. In the same way too you will recognize them by what they produce.

Notes.

The word usually translated "Jews" has 2 different senses: Judean and Jewish, Judean referring to the geographical area of Judea, and Jewish to the people who used to be called Israelites, the descendants of Jacob, place of abode being irrelevant. There are not separate words, and one can only judge from the context. In the New Testament, "Jewish" is more common than "Judean", and John (the writer of the Gospel) also uses the word *Ioudaioi* to refer to those Jewish and Judean leaders who opposed Jesus. It is generally agreed that he is using metonymy, using a part to describe a whole, but the question is whether in his use of metonymy he is referring to Jews or Judeans. Some argue that he is using *Ioudaioi* in the meaning "Judean" stating that it is more probable for him as he was a Jew. Others argue that in John 7:1 and 11:8 the word *Ioudaioi* does not refer to Jews or Judeans but means "Jewish leaders" / "Jewish authorities." It is not always easy to determine from the context when John is referring to certain Jewish leaders antagonistic to Jesus, leaders who happened to be concentrated in Jerusalem (which in turn, is in Judea), or when he is referring to Judeans or Jews in general.

There are 3 schools of thought on the meaning of the word often translated as "Jews." The majority view is that it means Jew and sometimes a special category of Jews (e.g. the leaders). Another viewpoint suggests that it is connected with the Roman province of Judea and can on occasion mean "Jew." The third point of view is that it means the ten tribes of the former Realm of Judea who did not retain the religion of the other two tribes.

Metonymy is also to be taken account in the case of the Pharisees. In the New Testament, it is important to note that not all Pharisees opposed Jesus, nor did Jesus take exception to all Pharisees – it was certain Pharisees only.

44. Gospel of Thomas.
Coptic
44) Jesus said, "Whoever blasphemes against the Father will be forgiven, and whoever blasphemes against the Son will be forgiven, but whoever blasphemes against the Holy Spirit will not be forgiven either on earth or in heaven."

New Testament.
Matthew 12:32.

If you speak against the Human Being, you will be forgiven for it, but if you speak against the Holy Spirit, you will not be forgiven for it, neither in this age nor in the age to come.

Mark 3:28-29.

All people groups will be forgiven for all their sins and any blasphemies they speak, but the person who blasphemes against the Holy Spirit will never be forgiven, but is guilty of an eternal sin."

Luke 12:10.

Anyone who says anything against the Human Being will be forgiven, but someone who blasphemes against the Holy Spirit will not be forgiven.

45. Gospel of Thomas.
Coptic
45) Jesus said, "Grapes are not harvested from thorns, nor are figs gathered from thistles, as they do not produce fruit. A good person brings good out of their storehouse, but a bad person brings out bad things from their bad storehouse, which is in their heart, and says bad things. A bad person brings out bad things out of the abundance of the heart."

New Testament.
Matthew 7:16-20.

You will have no trouble recognizing them by the consequences of their actions. Does anyone pick grapes from thorn bushes, or figs from thistles? Nice fruit grows on good trees, but evil fruit grows on rotten trees. Evil fruit can't grow on a good tree, and nice fruit can't grow on a rotten tree. Every tree that doesn't produce nice fruit is cut down and thrown into the fire. In the same way too you will recognize them by what they produce.

Luke 6:43-46.
"A good tree doesn't grow bad fruit, and a bad tree doesn't grow good fruit. Every tree is known by its own fruit! People do not pick[58] figs from thorn bushes, or bunches of grapes from bramble bushes. "A good person produces good things out of the good stored up in them, and an evil person produces evil things out of the evil stored up in them. The mouth speaks from the overflow of what is stored up in someone.[59]

Matthew 12: 33-37.
"You know whether a tree is or good or bad by the fruit it produces. If you grow a good tree you will have good fruit, but if you grow a bad tree you will have bad fruit. You pack of snakes! How can you, being evil, speak good things? The mouth speaks those things which overflow from the mind. A good person hurls out good things out of the good stored up in them, and an evil person hurls out evil things out of the evil stored up in them. It's a fact that people will have to give an account of every nonworking word on the Day of Judgment –for by your words you will have your rights claimed for you, and by your words you will be condemned!"

46. Gospel of Thomas.
Coptic
46) Jesus said, "Among those born of women, from Adam until John the Baptist, there is no one so superior to John the Baptist that his eyes should not be lowered before him. However, I have said whichever one of you becomes a child will be acquainted with the Realm and will become superior to John."

New Testament.
Matthew 11:11.
I tell you, no human in history has been more important than John the Baptizer! Yet the most insignificant person in Heaven's Realm is more important than he!

Luke 7:28.

I tell you, no human in history has been more important than John the Baptizer! Yet the most insignificant person in God's Realm is more important than he!"

Matthew 18:2-4.

Jesus called a child over, and put the child[60] down in the middle of them. He said, "Let me emphasize this, unless you change and become like children, there is no way you will enter Heaven's Realm! The person who brings themselves down to the level[61] of this child is greater in Heaven's Realm.

47. Gospel of Thomas.
Coptic

47) Jesus said, "It is impossible for a man to mount two horses or to stretch two bows. It is impossible for a servant to serve two masters, as he will honor one and treat the other disrespectfully. No one drinks old wine and immediately wishes to drink new wine. New wine is not put into old wineskins, as in that case they would they burst. Old wine is not put into a new wineskin, as it would spoil it. An old patch is not sewn onto a new piece of clothing, because a tear would result."

New Testament.
Matthew 6:24.

No one can be the slave servant[62] of two masters; then they would hate one and love the other, or alternatively would be loyal to the one and despise the other. You are not able to serve both God and wealth.[63]

Matthew 9:16-17.

And no one mends clothes with a patch of unshrunken cloth, because the patch will shrink and make an even worse tear. No one puts new wine into old wineskins. That makes the wineskins burst. Then the wine is spilled, and the wineskins are ruined. Instead, they put new wine into new wineskins, and both are safe."

Mark 2:21-22.

No one sews a patch of unshrunken cloth on an old coat. If they do, the added piece will tear away from the old one and make the tear worse. **22** And no one pours new wine into old wineskins. If they do, the wine will burst the skins, and then both the wine and the wineskins will be ruined. No, they pour new wine into fresh[64] wineskins."

Luke 5:26-39.

He also told them this example: "No one tears a piece from a new coat and puts it on an old one. Otherwise, not only will the new coat be torn, but the patch from the new won't match the old. **37** No one puts new wine into old wineskins. That makes the wineskins burst. Then the wine is spilled, and the wineskins are ruined. **38** Instead, they put new wine into new wineskins. **39** And no one who has drunk old wine wants new wine. They say, 'Old wine's good!'"

48. Gospel of Thomas.
Coptic

48) Jesus said, "If two make peace with each other in the one house, they will say to the mountain, 'Move Away,' and it will move away."

New Testament.
Matthew 18:19.

Let me make this quite clear, if two of you agree about anything that you ask, my Father in the heavenly places will do it for you.

Matthew 17:20.

"Because you don't have much faith!" he answered. "Let me make this clear, if you have faith like a mustard seed, you will say to this mountain, 'Move from here to there,' and it will move, and nothing will be impossible for you!'"[65]

Mark 11:23.

"Whoever says to this mountain, 'Be snatched up[66] and thrown into the sea,' and is not undecided,[67] but believes that what they say is happening, will have what they want.

49. Gospel of Thomas.
Coptic

49) Jesus said, "Blessed are the solitary and chosen, for you will find the Realm. For you are from it, and to it you will return."

50. Gospel of Thomas.
Coptic

50) Jesus said, "If they ask you, 'Where did you come from?', say to them, 'We came from the light, the place where the light came into being by itself and established itself and became visible through their image.'

If they ask you, 'Is it you?', say, 'We are its children; we are the chosen of the Living Father.' If they ask you, 'What is the sign of your father in you?', say to them, 'It is movement and restfulness.'"

51. Gospel of Thomas.
Coptic

51) His disciples said to him, "When will the resting of the dead happen, and when will the new world come?"

He said to them, "What you look forward to has already come, but you do not recognize it."

52. Gospel of Thomas.
Coptic

52) His disciples said to him, "Twenty-four prophets spoke in Israel, and all of them spoke through you."

He said to them, "You have omitted the one living in your presence and have spoken only of the dead."

53. Gospel of Thomas.
Coptic

53) His disciples said to him, "Is circumcision beneficial or not?"

He said to them, "If it were beneficial, their father would sire them already circumcised from their mother. Rather, it is true spiritual circumcision that has become completely beneficial."

54. Gospel of Thomas.
Coptic
54) Jesus said, "Blessed are the financially poor, for yours is Heaven's Realm.

New Testament.
Matthew 5:3.
He taught as follows: "The financially poor[68] are spiritually happy, because theirs is Heaven's Realm.

Luke 6:20.
Jesus looked at his disciples and said, "Happy are the financially poor, because yours is God's Realm.

55. Gospel of Thomas.
Coptic
55) Jesus said, "Whoever puts their father and mother first cannot become a disciple to me. Whoever puts their brothers and sisters first and does not take up their cross in my way will not be worthy of me."

New Testament.
Luke 14:26.
"No one can be my disciple if they put their father, mother, wife or children - even their own life – before me.[69]

Matthew 10:37-38.
Anyone who puts their father or mother first, before me, isn't worthy of me. Anyone who puts their son or daughter first, before me, isn't worthy of me. And anyone who doesn't pick up their cross and follow me isn't worthy of me!

56. Gospel of Thomas.
Coptic
56) Jesus said, "Whoever has come to understand the world has found a corpse, and whoever has found a corpse is superior to the world."

57. Gospel of Thomas.
Coptic

57) Jesus said, "The Father's Realm is like a person who had good seed. His enemy came by night and sowed weeds among the good seed. The person did not allow them to pull up the weeds, but said, 'I am afraid that you will intend to pull up the weeds but will pull up the grain along with them.' For on the day of the harvest, the weeds will be plainly visible, and they will be pulled up and burned."

New Testament.
Matthew 13:24-30.

Then Jesus set another example in front of them. "This is a story about Heaven's Realm. A farmer sowed good seed in his field. While everyone was asleep, his enemy planted troublesome weeds in the middle of the wheat then ran away. When the grain had sprouted[70] and produced a crop, then the troublesome weeds appeared too. The owner's workers asked, 'Sir, didn't you sow good seed in your field? So why does it have troublesome weeds?'

"'An enemy did this!' he answered.

"The servants asked, 'Do you want us to go and rip out the weeds?'

"'No," he replied, "in case while you're in the process of ripping out the weeds you accidentally uproot the wheat at the same time. **30** Let both of them grow together until the harvest. Then at harvest time I'll tell the harvesters to collect the weeds first and tie them in bundles so they can be burned up, but to collect the wheat and put it in my barn."

58. Gospel of Thomas.
Coptic

58) Jesus said, "Blessed is the person who has suffered and found life."

59. Gospel of Thomas.
Coptic

59) Jesus said, "Pay attention to the Living One while you are alive, in case you die and wish to see him but are unable to do so."

New Testament.
John 7:34.
You will look for me and not be able to find me, and where I am going, you can't come!

John 13:33.
My dear little members,[71] I'll be with you a little while longer. You will look for me, and what I told the Jews, I'm telling you now: where I'm going, you can't come.

60. Gospel of Thomas.
Coptic
60) They saw a Samaritan carrying a lamb on his way to Judea. He said to his disciples, "Why does that man carry the lamb around?"

They said to him, "So that he can kill it and eat it."

He said to them, "While it is alive, he will not eat it, but only after he has killed it and it has become a corpse."

They said to him, "He can do nothing else."

He said to them, "You too, look for a place for yourself within the Restfulness, in case you become a corpse and are eaten."

61. Gospel of Thomas.
Coptic
61) Jesus said, "Two will rest on a bed. One will die, and other will live."

Salome said to him, "Hey you, who are you, that you, as though from the One, have come up on my dining couch and eaten from my table?"

Jesus said to her, "I am he who exists from the Undivided. I was given some of my Father's things."

Salome said, "I am your disciple."

Jesus said to her, "Then I say, if he is undivided, he will be filled with light, but if he is divided, he will be filled with darkness."

New Testament.
Luke 17:34.
On that night two people will be on one bed - one will be taken and the other one left.

62. Gospel of Thomas.
Coptic

62) Jesus said, "It is to those who are worthy of my secret hidden truths that I tell my mysteries. Do not let your left hand know what your right hand is doing."

New Testament.
Matthew 6:3.

When you do a charitable deed, keep it to yourself and don't tell anyone. **4** Make sure it's a secret. And your Father who is watching you in secret will reward you.[72]

Matthew 13:11.

He answered, "You are permitted to know the secret hidden truths of Heaven's Realm, but they are not permitted to know.

Mark 4:11-12.

"The hidden secret of God's Realm has been given to you," he answered, "but everything is said in examples to those on the outside with the result that, 'They look but they do not see. They hear but don't put two and two together. Otherwise they would turn to God and be forgiven.'"

Luke 8:10.

He explained, "You are permitted to know the secret hidden truths of God's Realm, but to others I speak in examples, so that, 'Although they see,[73] they do not observe. Although they hear, they do not understand.'[74]

Note.

The word translated "mysteries" properly meant secret hidden truths shown only to initiates. These days in the English language of our time, "mysteries" has taken on a different meaning.

63. Gospel of Thomas.
Coptic

63) Jesus said, "There was a rich person who had a great deal of money. He said, 'I will put my money to use. I will sow, reap, plant, and fill my storehouse with produce, and the result will be

that I will lack nothing.' These were his intentions, but that same night he died. If you have ears you had better listen!"

New Testament.
Luke 12:16-21.

He told them the following example. "A certain rich person's farm produced a good crop. He thought to himself, 'What am I to do? I don't have anywhere to store my crops!' Then he said, 'I know what I'll do. I'll pull down my barns and build bigger ones, and I'll store all my grain and other possessions there. Then I can say to myself, "You have enough good things stored up to last for ages. Take it easy - eat, drink, and party on."' But God said to him, 'You silly fool! Tonight you're going to die. And then who's going to get everything that you've stored up!' And this will be the case with anyone who stores up things for their own use but is not wealthy in God's way."[75]

64. Gospel of Thomas.
Coptic

64) Jesus said, "A person received guests. When he had prepared the dinner, he sent his servant to invite guests. He went to the first one and said to him, "My master invites you.'

He replied, 'I have claims against some merchants. They are coming to me this evening. I must go and give them my orders. I ask to be excused from the dinner.' He went to another and said, 'My master has invited you.' He replied, 'I have just bought a house and am required for the day. I do not have any spare time.' He went to another and said to him, 'My master invites you.' He replied, 'My friend is going to get married, and I have to prepare the feast. I will not be able to come. I ask to be excused from the dinner.' He went to another and said to him, 'My master invites you.' He replied, 'I have just bought a farm, and I'm on my way to collect the rent. I won't be able to come. I ask to be excused.' The servant returned and said to his master, 'Those whom you invited to the dinner have asked to be excused.'

The master said to his servant, 'Go outside to the streets and bring back anyone you happen to meet; invite them to dine.' Businessmen and merchants will not enter my Father's places."

New Testament.
Matthew 22:3-9.

"He sent his slave servants to call the invited guests to the wedding but they didn't want to come. Next he sent other slave servants with the instructions, 'Tell the invited guests, "I have prepared the feast – all the meat is ready! Everything is ready! Come to the wedding."'"

"But they couldn't care less, and they went away. One went to his own farm, another went to his business, but the rest of them grabbed his slave servants and beat them up badly, killing them. The king was furious and sent his armies. They destroyed those murderers and burned down their city. Then the king said to his slave servants, 'The wedding is ready, but the invited guests weren't worthy of the honor. So go out to the highways and invite anyone you find to the wedding.'

Luke 14:16-24.

But Jesus answered, "A certain person was organizing a big party and invited a lot of guests. When the party was ready a slave servant was sent to tell the guests, 'Come on, everything's ready now.'[76] But every one of them began to make excuses.[77] The first one said, 'I've just bought some land, and I have to go and see it. Please accept my apologies.' Another one said, 'I've just bought five pair of oxen, and I'm on my way to try them out. Please accept my apologies.' Still another one said, 'I just got married, so I really can't come.'

"The servant came back and reported all this to the boss. Then the owner of the house became angry and ordered the slave servant, 'Hurry out into the streets and alleys of the city and bring in the financially poor, the disabled, the blind and the crippled.' After that happened, the servant said, 'Master, I've done what you said, but there's still some room.' Then the master told the servant, 'Go out into the roads and country lanes and make them come in - I want my house to be full.' I tell you, not one of those invited guests will get so much as a taste of the feast!"

65. Gospel of Thomas.
Coptic

65) He said, "There was a good person who owned a vineyard. He leased it to tenant farmers so that they would work it and he would collect the produce from them. He sent his servant to collect the vineyard's produce from the tenants. They seized his servant and beat him, all but killing him. The servant went back and told his master. The master said, 'Perhaps they didn't recognize him.' He sent another servant. The tenants beat this one as well. Then the owner sent his son and said, 'Perhaps they will show respect to my son.' The tenants knew he was the heir to the vineyard, so they seized him and killed him. If you have ears you had better listen!"

New Testament.
Matthew 21:33-41.

"Listen to another example. There was a certain person, a landowner, who planted a vineyard and put a hedge around it, dug a wine press in it and built a tower. He leased it out to farmers and set out on a journey. When vintage time got close, he sent his slave servants to the farmers to collect its fruit. **35** The farmers grabbed his slave servants, beat one, killed one and stoned another. Next he sent other slave servants, more than the first, and they did the same to them. Last of all he sent his son to them. 'They will respect my son!' he said to himself. But when the farmers saw the son, they said to each other 'This is the heir! Come on, let's kill him and get the inheritance!'

"They grabbed him, threw him out of the vineyard and murdered him. So then, when the owner of the vineyard comes, what's he going to do to those farmers?"

They answered, "He will see to it that those bad people have a horrible death. Then he will lease the vineyard to other farmers who will give him his share of each harvest."

Mark 12:1-8.

Jesus began speaking to them in examples: "A person planted a vineyard, put a fence[78] around it, dug a pit for the wine vat and built a tower.[79] Then he leased it to some farmers and went to a far away country. At vintage time he sent a slave servant to the farmers to collect some of the vineyard produce from the farmers. They grabbed him, tanned his hide and sent him packing[80] empty handed. So the vineyard owner sent another slave servant. They banged him on the head,[81] insulted him and sent him packing. Again he sent another slave servant, and they killed him. He sent many more slave servants, and they killed some and beat the others up. Now he still had one son who he loved. He sent him to them last of all, thinking, 'They will respect my son!' But these farmers said to each other, 'This is the heir – come on, let's kill him, and then we'll get the inheritance!' So they grabbed him, killed him and hurled him out of the vineyard.

Luke 20:9-15.

Jesus went on to tell the people this example: "There was a certain person who planted a vineyard, then rented it out to some farmers and went away from home for a long time. At harvest time the owner sent a slave servant to the farmers to collect some of the vineyard's produce. But the farmers beat him up and sent him away empty-handed. So he sent another servant, but they also beat him up and insulted him and sent him away empty-handed. Then he sent a third servant, but they injured him and threw him out. Then the owner of the vineyard said, 'What am I going to do? I'll send my own dear son, perhaps they will respect him!' But when the farmers saw him, they discussed the matter. They said, 'This is the heir – let's kill him, then the inheritance will be ours!' So they threw him out of the vineyard and killed him.

66. Gospel of Thomas.
Coptic

66) Jesus said, "Show me the stone which the builders have rejected. That one is the cornerstone."

New Testament.

Matthew 21:42.

Jesus said to them, "Haven't you ever read in the Scriptures, 'The stone which the builders rejected has become the cornerstone; this was done by the Lord, and it is wonderful to see!'"?[82]

Mark 12:10-11.

Haven't you read the Scripture, 'The stone which the builders rejected has become the cornerstone. This was done by the Lord, and it is wonderful to see!

Luke 20:17.

Then Jesus looked straight at them and said, "So then what is the meaning of the Scripture: 'The stone which the builders rejected has become the cornerstone?'[83]

67. Gospel of Thomas.
Coptic

67) Jesus said, "Whoever believes that the All itself is deficient is completely deficient."

68. Gospel of Thomas.
Coptic

68) Jesus said, "You are blessed when you are hated and persecuted. Wherever you have been persecuted they will find no place."

New Testament.

Matthew 5:11.

Happy are you whenever they heap insults on you, and persecute you and tell all kinds of evil lies about you because of me.

Luke 6:22.

Happy are you when people hate you, when they banish[84] you and insult you and reject your name with contempt as if it's evil, because of the Human Being.

69. Gospel of Thomas.
Coptic

69) Jesus said, "Blessed are they who have been persecuted within themselves. It is they who have truly come to know the Father. Blessed are the hungry, for the belly of the one who hungers will be filled."

New Testament.
Matthew 5:6-8.

Happy are those who hunger and thirst to be just, because they will have their fill. Happy are the merciful, because they will obtain mercy. Happy are those with purified minds, because they will see God.

Luke 6:21.

Happy are you who are hungry now, for you will be have your fill. Happy are you who cry now, for you will laugh.

70. Gospel of Thomas.
Coptic

70) Jesus said, "If you bring forth what is within you, what you bring forth will save you. If you do not bring forth what is within you, that which you do not bring forth will destroy you."

71. Gospel of Thomas.
Coptic

71) Jesus said, "I will destroy this house, and no one will be able to rebuild it."

New Testament.
Mark 14:58.

"We heard him say, 'I will destroy this human-built temple and will build another one in three days, one that hasn't been made by people.'"

72. Gospel of Thomas.
Coptic

72) Someone said to him, "Tell my brothers to divide my father's possessions with me."

He said to him, "Hey you, who has made me a divider?"

He turned to his disciples and said to them, "I'm not a divider, am I?"

New Testament.
Luke 12:13-15.

Then someone in the crowd asked, "Teacher, please tell my brother to divide the inheritance with me."

Jesus said, "Hey, who appointed me the judge over the two of you or the executor of the will!" Then he said to them, "Watch out! Beware of all types of greedy grasping behavior - your life is not made up by a lot of possessions!"

73. Gospel of Thomas.
Coptic
73) Jesus said, "There is a big harvest but the laborers are few. Put a request to the master to send out laborers to the harvest."

New Testament.
Matthew 9:37-38.
Then he said to his disciples, "On the one hand there's a big harvest, but on the other hand there are not enough workers. So then put a request to the Harvest Master so that he will throw workers into his harvest!"

Luke 10:2.
He said to them, "On the one hand there's a big harvest, but on the other hand there are not enough workers. Put some effort into it! Ask the Harvest Master to throw workers into his harvest!"[85]

74. Gospel of Thomas.
Coptic
74) He said, "Lord, there are many around the drinking trough, but there is nothing in the cistern."

75. Gospel of Thomas.
Coptic
75) Jesus said, "Many are standing at the door, but it is the solitary who will enter the bridal chamber."

New Testament.
Matthew 22:14.
Many are invited but few are chosen!

Matthew 25:1-13.
"This is also a story about Heaven's Realm. Ten unmarried girls[86] took their lamps and went out to meet the bridegroom.[87]

There were five silly ones and five sensible ones. The silly ones didn't take any oil with their lamps. On the other hand, the wise ones took oil containers with their lamps. The bridegroom was away a long time, so they all got tired and went to sleep.

"At midnight there was a shout, 'Here's the bridegroom! Go out and meet him!'

"Then all the girls got up and got their lamps ready. The silly ones said to the wise ones, 'Give us some of your oil! Our lamps are going out!'

"But the wise ones answered, 'No, if we do that, we might not have enough! Go away and buy your own!'

"The bridegroom came while they were away buying it. Everyone who was ready went with him to the wedding and the door was shut. Afterwards the other girls came too, and said, 'Sir, sir, open the door!'

"But he answered, 'I tell you I don't know you!'

"So then keep your wits about you, because you don't know the day nor the hour.

76. Gospel of Thomas.
Coptic
76) Jesus said, "The Realm of the Father is like a merchant who had a consignment of merchandise and who discovered a pearl. The merchant was astute. He sold the merchandise and bought solely the pearl for himself. You too, seek his reliable and continuing treasure where no moth approaches to devour and no worm destroys."

New Testament.
Matthew 6:20.
Don't put your wealth in a bank for yourselves on earth, where moths and rust can destroy it and where thieves can break in and steal it! Instead, put your wealth in a bank in heaven, where moths and rust don't destroy it, and thieves don't break in and steal it.

Matthew 13:45-46.
This is a story about Heaven's Realm. It is like a merchant searching for beautiful pearls. When he had found one expensive pearl, he sold everything that he had to buy it.

Luke 12:33.

Sell your possessions and give charitable gifts. Make for yourselves money bags that never wear out, a bank in the heavenly places that never fails, where there are no thieves to steal it nor clothes-moths to eat it.

77, 30/77. Gospel of Thomas.
Coptic

77) Jesus said, "It is I who am the light which is above them all. It is I who am the All. From me the All came forth, and the All extended to me. Split a piece of wood, and I am there. Lift up the stone, and you will find me there."

Greek

30/77) Jesus said: "Where there are two, they are not without God, and when there is one alone, I say, I am with him. Raise the stone, and you will find me there. Split the wood, and I am there."

New Testament.
John 1:1-5.

In the beginning was the Word, and the Word stayed with God, and the Word was God. In the beginning the Word stayed with[88] God. Everything came into being through him, and nothing came into being without him. That which came into being, life, was by means of him, and the life was the light of humans. And the light shines in the darkness, and the darkness did not suppress it.[89]

John 8:12.

When Jesus spoke to them again, he said, "I am the light of the world. Whoever follows me will never walk around in the dark, but will have light shining on their life."

78. Gospel of Thomas.
Coptic

78) Jesus said, "Why have you come out into the desert? To see a skinny plant blowing around in the wind? To see a man clothed in fine clothes like your kings and your important people? They are wearing fancy clothes, and they are unable to discern the truth."

New Testament.

Matthew 11:7-9.

After John's disciples left, Jesus started telling the crowds about John. "What did you expect to see when you went out into the wilderness? A skinny plant blowing around in the wind? What did you expect to see? A person wearing fancy clothes? No way! People who wear fancy clothes live in palaces. What did you expect to see? A prophet? That's right, and he's more than a prophet.

Luke 7:24-26.

After John's messengers left, Jesus began to speak to the crowd about John: "What did you expect to see when you went out into the wilderness? A skinny plant blowing around in the wind? What did you expect to see? A person wearing fancy clothes? No way! People who wear fancy clothes live in palaces. What did you expect to see? A prophet? That's right, and he's more than a prophet.

79. Gospel of Thomas.
Coptic

79) A woman from the crowd said to him, "Blessed are the womb which bore you and the breasts which nourished you."

He replied, "Blessed are those who have heard the word of the Father and have truly kept it. There will be days when you will say, 'Blessed are the womb which has never conceived and the breasts which have never given milk.'"

New Testament.

Luke 11:27-28.

As Jesus was saying this, a woman called out from the crowd, "Happy is the woman who was pregnant with you and breast-fed you."

Jesus said, "That may be true, but happy are those who hear God's Word and guard it."

Luke 23:28-29.

Jesus turned and said to them, "Daughters of Jerusalem, don't cry over me, cry for yourselves and for your children, because the time will come when you'll say, 'Happy are women who have never had children, wombs that were never pregnant, and breasts that never breastfed!

80. Gospel of Thomas.
Coptic
80) Jesus said, "The one who has recognized the world has found the body, but the one who has found the body is superior to the world."

81. Gospel of Thomas.
Coptic
81) Jesus said, "Let the one who has grown rich be king, and let the one who possesses power renounce it."

82. Gospel of Thomas.
Coptic
82) Jesus said, "The one who is near me is near the fire, and the one who is far from me is far from the Realm."

83. Gospel of Thomas.
Coptic
83) Jesus said, "The images are visible to humans, but the light in them remains concealed in the image of the Father's light. He will become visible, but his image will remain concealed by his light."

84. Gospel of Thomas.
Coptic
84) Jesus said, "When you see your likeness, you celebrate, but when you see your images which came into being before you, and which do not die or become visible, how much you will have to bear!"

85. Gospel of Thomas.
Coptic
85) Jesus said, "Adam came into being from a great power and a great wealth, but he did not become worthy of you. If he had he been worthy, he would not have experienced death."

86. Gospel of Thomas.
Coptic
86) Jesus said, "The foxes have their holes and the birds have their nests, but the Human Being has no place to lay his head and rest."

New Testament.
Matthew 8:20.
"Foxes have dens and birds have nests," Jesus replied, "but the Human Being[90] doesn't have anywhere to stay for the night!"[91]

Luke 9:58.
"Foxes have holes and birds of the air have nests," Jesus replied, "but the Human Being has nowhere to stay tonight."[92]

87. Gospel of Thomas.
Coptic
87) Jesus said, "The body that is dependant on a body is miserable, and the soul that is dependent on these two is miserable."

88. Gospel of Thomas.
Coptic
88) Jesus said, "The angels and the prophets will come to you and give you the things you already have. You too, give them the things which you have, and say to yourselves, 'When will they come and take what is theirs?'"

89. Gospel of Thomas.
Coptic
89) Jesus said, "Why do you wash the outside of the cup? Don't you realize that the one who made the inside is the same one who made the outside?"

New Testament.
Luke 11:39-40.
The Lord said to him, "As a matter of fact you Pharisees clean the outside of the cup and dish, but inside you are full of greed and wickedness. You silly twits! Didn't God make both the outside and the inside!

90. Gospel of Thomas.
Coptic
90) Jesus said, "Come to me. My yoke is gentle and my lordship is mild, and you will find rest for yourselves."

New Testament.
Matthew 11:28-30.
If you are tired and weighed down, come to me and have a rest! Harness up, with me at the reins, and learn from me. I am gentle and kind, and you will have a break from work. I harness you up with kindness and don't weigh you down."

91. Gospel of Thomas.
Coptic
91) They said to him, "Tell us who you are so that we may believe you."
He replied, "You read the features of the sky and the earth, but you have not recognized the one who is before you, and you do not know how to read this moment."

New Testament.
John 9:36.
The person asked, "Who is he, sir? Tell me so I can place my faith in him."

Luke 12:54-56.
He said to the crowd, "When you see a cloud coming up in the west, you immediately say, 'It's going to rain'- and it does! When the south wind comes up, you say, 'It's going to be hot' - and it is! You overly critical, hair splitting, pedantic, religious types! You know how to interpret the appearance of the earth and the sky. So why is it that you don't know how to interpret the times you're in?

92. Gospel of Thomas.
Coptic
92) Jesus said, "Seek and you will find. Yet, what you asked me about in former times and which I did not tell you then, I now do wish to tell you, but you do not ask about it."

New Testament.
Matthew 7:7.
Ask and it will be given to you, seek and you will find, knock and the door will be opened for you.

93. Gospel of Thomas.
Coptic
93) Jesus said, "Do not give what is sacred to dogs, because they will throw them on the manure pile. Do not throw the pearls to swine, or they will grind them to bits."

New Testament.
Matthew 7:6.
Don't give anything sacred to dogs or throw your pearls in front of pigs, because they'll crush them underfoot and tear you to pieces!

94. Gospel of Thomas.
Coptic
94) Jesus said, "The one who seeks will find, and the one who knocks will be let in."

New Testament.
Matthew 7:7.
Ask and it will be given to you, seek and you will find, knock and the door will be opened for you.

Luke 11:9-10.
Ask[93] and it will be given to you, seek and you will find, knock and the door will be opened for you. Everyone who asks receives, and everyone who seeks finds, and the door will be opened for the person who knocks.

95. Gospel of Thomas.
Coptic
95) Jesus said, "If you have money, do not lend it at interest, but give it to one from whom you will not get it back."

New Testament.
Luke 6:34-35.

If you lend to those people whom you expect to repay you, is that a big deal? Even sinners lend to sinners, and expect to be repaid the whole amount! **35** Instead, love your enemies, be good to people and lend. Don't expect anything in return, and you will have a big reward, and you will be children of the Most High. He is kind to the ungrateful and evil.

Luke 14:12-14.

Then Jesus also said to his host, "When you have lunch or dinner, don't invite your friends, associates, relatives, or your rich neighbors. If you do, they'll invite you back and you'll be repaid. But when you give a party, invite the poor, the disabled, the crippled,[94] and the blind, and you will be blessed! Although they can't repay you, you will be repaid at the resurrection of the just."

96. Gospel of Thomas.
Coptic

96) Jesus said, "The Father's Realm is like a certain woman. She took a little leaven, concealed it in some dough, and made it into large loaves. If you have ears you had better listen!"

New Testament.
Matthew 13:33.

He told them another example. "This is a story about Heaven's Realm. A woman took some yeast and baked it in three lumps of dough, and then all the bread rose."

Luke 13:20-21.

Again he asked, "To what can I compare God's Realm? It is like yeast that a woman took and hid into three batches of flour until all the bread rose."

97. Gospel of Thomas.
Coptic

97) Jesus said, "The Father's Realm is like a certain woman who was carrying a jar full of meal. While she was walking down a road, still a distance from home, the jar's handle broke and the meal

emptied out behind her on the road. She did not realize it as she had not noticed the accident. When she reached her house, she put the jar down and found it empty."

98. Gospel of Thomas.
Coptic
98) Jesus said, "The Father's Realm is like a certain person who wanted to kill a powerful person. He drew his sword in his own house and stuck it into the wall in order to find out whether his hand could carry through. Then he killed the powerful person."

99. Gospel of Thomas.
Coptic
99) The disciples said to him, "Your brothers and your mother are standing outside."

He said to them, "Those here who do the will of my Father are my brothers and my mother. It is they who will enter my Father's Realm.

New Testament.
Matthew 12:46-50.

While Jesus was still speaking to the crowds, his mother and siblings[95] were standing outside, wanting to speak with him. Someone said to him, "Hey there, your mother and siblings are standing outside. They want to speak with you."

Who is my mother and who are my siblings?" Jesus asked. He pointed to his disciples and said, "Here are my mother and my siblings! Whoever does the purpose of my Father in the heavenly places is indeed my brother, and sister, and mother."

Mark 3:31-35.

Jesus' mother and siblings[96] arrived. They stood outside and sent someone in to call him. There was a crowd sitting around him, and they told him, "Your mother, brothers, and sisters are outside looking for you."

"Who are my mother and siblings?" he asked. He looked around at those sitting in a circle around him, and said, "These are my mother and siblings! Whoever does God's purpose is my brother, sister, and mother."

100. Gospel of Thomas.
Coptic
100) They showed Jesus a gold coin and said to him, "Caesar's men demand taxes from us."

He said to them, "Give Caesar what belongs to Caesar, give God what belongs to God, and give me what belongs to me."

New Testament.
Mark 12:13-17.

They sent some Pharisees and some friends and supporters of Herod Antipas to Jesus, to bait a hook[97] for him on what he said. When they arrived, they said to him, "Teacher, we know that you're sincere and don't concern yourself about anyone's opinion, as you don't go by outward appearances, but teach the way of God with all sincerity. So is it legal to pay the Roman poll-tax[98] to Caesar or not? Are we to pay, or not to pay?"

But Jesus, knowing they were overly critical, hair-splitting, pedantic religious[99] types, asked, "Why are you putting me to the test? Bring a Roman coin for me to look at!"

So they brought it, and Jesus asked, "Whose portrait is this? Whose inscription is it?"

"Caesar's!" they said.

"Give back[100] to Caesar what belongs to Caesar," Jesus remarked, "and give back to God what belongs to God." And they were completely shocked by him.

Luke 20:21-25.

So the spies put a question to him, "Teacher, we know what you speak and teach is correct, and that you don't take people on face value, but teach the truth about God's way. So is it legal to pay taxes to Caesar, or not?"

Jesus saw through their cunning and said, "Show me a silver coin.[101] Whose face and inscription are on it?"

"Caesar's!" they answered.

"Give back to Caesar what belongs to Caesar," Jesus said, "and give back to God what belongs to God!"

101. Gospel of Thomas.
Coptic

101) Jesus said, "Whoever does puts his father and his mother first, which I do not, cannot become my disciple. Whoever does not love his father and his mother as I do cannot become my disciple. My mother gave birth to me, but my true Mother gave me life."

New Testament.
Matthew 10:37.

Anyone who puts their father or mother first, before me, isn't worthy of me. Anyone who puts their son or daughter first, before me, isn't worthy of me.

Luke 14:26.

No one can be my disciple if they put their father, mother, wife or children - even their own life – before me.

Notes.

Miseo, "hate," is not always as strong as, and has a wider meaning than, the English word "hate". For example, Homer uses it in the sense "Zeus hated (did not allow) that he should become a prey to the enemy dogs of Troy", Iliad 17.272, and Aristophanes uses it in the sense "passion", "grudging" cf. Birds 36.

102. Gospel of Thomas.
Coptic

102) Jesus said, "Woe to the Pharisees, for they are like a dog sleeping in the oxen's manger. The dog does not eat nor does the dog let the oxen eat."

New Testament.
Matthew 23:13.

Woe to you, Bible scholars and Pharisees, you overly critical, hair splitting, pedantic religious types, because you shut people out of Heaven's Realm! You don't go in there yourself, and what's more, you stop other people from going in too!

103. Gospel of Thomas.
Coptic

103) Jesus said, "Fortunate is the person who knows where the robbers will enter, so that he can get up, assemble his domain, and arm himself before they attack."

New Testament.
Matthew 24:43.

Realize this, that if the owner of the household had known the time of the night the thief would come, they would have kept their wits about them and not allowed their house to be broken into.

Luke 12:39.

But understand this - if the owner of the house had known what time the thief was coming, he wouldn't have let his house be broken in to.

104. Gospel of Thomas.
Coptic

104) They said to Jesus, "Come, let us pray today and let us fast."
Jesus said, "What is the sin that I have committed, or by which I have been defeated? When the bridegroom leaves the bridal chamber, then let them fast and pray."

105. Gospel of Thomas.
Coptic

105) Jesus said, "He who knows the father and the mother will be called a harlot's associate."

106. Gospel of Thomas.
Coptic

106) Jesus said, "When you make the two one, you will become humans, and when you say, 'Mountain, move away,' it will move away."

New Testament.
"Whoever says to this mountain, 'Be snatched up[102] and thrown into the sea,' and is not undecided,[103] but believes that what they say is happening, will have what they want."

107. Gospel of Thomas.
Coptic

107) Jesus said, "The Realm is like a shepherd who had a hundred sheep. The largest one of them wandered off. The shepherd left the ninety-nine sheep and searched for that one until he found it. After he had gone to such trouble, he said to the sheep, 'I care for you more than the ninety-nine.'"

New Testament.
Matthew 18:12-13.

What do you think? If someone has 100 sheep, and one of them wanders off,[104] don't they leave the 99 and go to the mountains to look for the one that's wandered off? And if they happen to find it, they are happier about it than the 99 that didn't wander off!

Luke 15:3-7.

But Jesus told them this example. "Suppose one of you has 100 sheep and you lose one of them. Surely you leave the other 99 in the open country and keep looking for the lost sheep until you find it! And when you find it, you're happy! You put it on your shoulders and go back home. Then you call your friends and neighbors and say, 'Come and celebrate - I've found that lost sheep!' In the same way there will be more celebrating in heaven over one sinner who changes their mind than over the other 99 people who are right with God who don't need to change their minds.

108. Gospel of Thomas.
Coptic

108) Jesus said, "He who will drink from my mouth will become like me. I myself will become he, and the things that are hidden will become revealed to him."

109. Gospel of Thomas.
Coptic

109) Jesus said, "The Realm is like a person who had a hidden treasure in his field without knowing it. After he died, his son inherited it. The son did not know about it. He inherited the field and sold it. The one who bought it plowed it and found the treasure. He began to lend money at interest to whomever he wished."

New Testament.
Matthew 13:44.

This is a story about Heaven's Realm. A person came across some treasure in a field, and hid it again there. They are so thrilled to find it that they sell everything they own to buy the field.

110. Gospel of Thomas.
Coptic
110) Jesus said, "Whoever finds the world and becomes rich, is to renounce the world."

111. Gospel of Thomas.
Coptic
111) Jesus said, "The heavens and the earth will be rolled up in your presence. The one who lives from the Living One will not see death."

Doesn't Jesus say, "Whoever finds himself is superior to the world?"

112. Gospel of Thomas.
Coptic
112) Jesus said, "Woe to the flesh that depends on the soul; woe to the soul that depends on the flesh."

113. Gospel of Thomas.
Coptic
113) His disciples asked him, "When will the Realm come?"
Jesus said, "It will not come by waiting for it. It will not be a matter of saying 'Here it is' or 'There it is.' Rather, the Father's Realm is spread out upon the earth, and people do not see it."

New Testament.
Luke 17:20-21.

Once Jesus was asked by the Pharisees when God's Realm would come. Jesus said, "God's Realm won't come just because you're watching for it, and neither can people say, 'Here it is!' or 'There it is', because God's Realm is actually within you!"

114. Gospel of Thomas.
Coptic

114) Simon Peter said to him, "Let Mary leave us, as women are not worthy of life."

Jesus said, "I myself will lead her in order to make her male, so that she too may become a living spirit resembling you males. For every woman who makes herself male will enter Heaven's Realm."

Chapter 7. Endnotes.

[1] Today the village of al-Bahnasa occupies part of the ancient site.

[2] R. Cameron, "Gospel of Thomas," *The Anchor Bible Dictionary*, ed. David Noel Freedman. New York: Doubleday, 1992, V. 6, p. 535.

[3] H. Köster, *Ancient Christian gospels: their history and development*, Trinity Press, Valley Forge, Pa., 1992, p. 77.

[4] B. Layton, *ed.* Gospel "According to Thomas, Gospel According to Philip, Hypostasis of the Archons, and Indexes." Nag Hammadi Studies 20: Nag Hammadi Codex II, 2-7. Vol. I, Leiden – New York – København – Köln: Brill.

[5] Eusebius, *Historia Ecclesiastica* III.39. 16.

[6] There is no evidence to suggest that Papias was Irenaeus' source. Later, Origen, Jerome, Augustine all stated that Matthew's gospel was originally written in Hebrew.

Note that there is not currently academic consensus as to whether these "sayings" of Matthew were the same work as the "gospel of Matthew" we have today.

[7] S. Davies, "Mark's Use of the Gospel of Thomas," *Neotestamentica: The Journal of the New Testament Society of South Africa*, 30 (2) 1996 pp. 307-334.

[8] See below.

[9] Eusebius, *Historia Ecclesiastica* V.8, 2.

[10] Some doubt the validity of Irenaeus' statement.

[11] And to Mark, Luke, Romans, 1 Corinthians, Ephesians, 1 Timothy, Titus, Hebrews, James, 1 Peter.

[12] Ignatius also refers to Mark, Luke, John, Acts, Romans, 1 Corinthians, 2 Corinthians, Galatians, Ephesians, Philippians, Colossians, 1 Thessalonians, 1 Timothy, 2 Timothy, Titus, Philemon, Hebrews, James, 1 Peter, 2 Peter, 1 John, 3 John, Revelation.

[13] In the sum of his works, Polycarp refers to Matthew, Mark, Luke, John, Acts, Romans, 1 Corinthians, 2 Corinthians , Galatians, Ephesians, Philippians, Colossians, 2 Thessalonians, 1 Timothy, 2 Timothy, Hebrews, 1 Peter, 1 John.

[14] Louise Wells, *op.cit.*, p. 130.

[15] Eusebius, *HE* 3.39.12-16.

[16] *Muratorian Canon, ll.* 2-3.

[17] "Tertium evangelii librum secundum Lucam. Lucas iste medicus post ascensum Christi, cum eum Paulus quasi ut iuris studiosum secum adsumpsisset, nomine suo ex opinione conscripsit, dominum tamen nec ipse vidit in carne."

[18] See the two prefaces: Luke 1:1-4 and Acts 1:1-2. Acts 1:1-5 recapitulates the conclusion of Luke 24:36-53. Some have compared this to Thucydides' second preface in his *History of the Peloponnesian War*, 5:26ff.

[19] A. Schmidt, "Zwel Anmerkungen zu P.Ryl. III 457", *Archiv fur Papyrusforschung*, 35 (1989) 11-12.

[20] See S.R. Pickering, *Recently Published New Testament Papyri: P89-P95*, (Macquarie: The Ancient History Documentary Research Centre, 1991). People also cite the Egerton papyrus as very early, but note Pickering's comment (p. 13): "A fresh source of doubt arises from Gronewald's re-dating (in P.Koln IV) of the Egerton-Cologne apocryphon to ca. 200."

[21] Irenaeus' testimony has been called into doubt.

[22] Clement of Alexandria, *Hypotyposes*, cited in Eusebius, *HE* 6.14.7.

[23] Both commonly, for example P.Coll.Youtie 67; CPR 14; BGU 2251.7; AE 419; BGU 2223.

[24] For example, CIJ 1.14, 30; CPJ I.126; CPJ II.178; CPJ III.462f; CPJ III.459.

[25] Ant. 1.240; 5.85; 12.43; 12.157; 13.188; 13.131; 13. 320; 13.383; 13.385; 13.420; 18.35.

[26] See H.C. Youtie, Scriptiunculae I (Amsterdam, 1973), esp. 330; P.M. Fraser, Ptolemaic Alexandria, II, (Oxford, 1972), esp. 116f; R. Calderini, Aeg. 21 (1941) 221-60; Aeg. 22 (1942) 3-45.

[27] See commentary by J.R. Rea, CPR 11.

[28] Horsley, G.H.R., ed., *New Documents Illustrating Early Christianity*, Vols 1-5, North Ryde, N.S.W., Macquarie University Ancient History Documentary Research Centre, 1982-1989 , 1.123.

[29] Here the Greek refers to individual seeds.

[30] The *ho men*, answered by the *kai eteron* at the beginning of v. 6.

[31] Isaiah 64:4.

[32] *Paradeisis*, commonly transliterated as "paradise", a Persian loan word meaning a garden of fruit trees (or orchard) which first occurs in Greek in Xenophon's *Anabasis*, 1.2.7. It appears commonly in the papyri and inscriptions in the same meaning. See *I.Tyre* 1.108 (pl.47.1) (late Roman), "I solemnly request those who are going to acquire this orchard…"; *P.Petr.* i.16.2.7 (230 B.C.), "the produce of my orchards"; *P.Tebt* 1.5.53 (118 B.C.), "the tithes which they used to receive from the holdings and the orchards". *P.Lond* 933.12 (A.D. 211) notes a payment on account of an "olive orchard". See also the Rosetta Stone (OGIS 90.15, 196 B.C.). It occurs frequently in the LXX as a garden, sometimes as the abode of the blessed, see Cant. 5.13, Eccl. 2.5, and Neh. 2.8. The Midrash Haggadah (Midrash means a verse-by-verse interpretation of Scripture, and Haggadah is an interpretation and expansion of the non-legal portions of Scripture) describes Paradise in detail, as far as giving specific dimensions and furnishings of the chambers. The details are supposed to have been supplied by individuals who visited Paradise while alive. It states that 9 mortals visited heaven while alive, and that one of these is Enoch. Enoch 20:7-8 states "Gabriel, one of the holy angels, who is over Paradise and the serpents and the Cherubim…", and supplies a description of Paradise in Chapters 23-38. Ezekiel's description of Paradise is similar: a great mountain in the middle of the earth which has streams of water flowing from under it. A palm tree grows in the middle of the center of the sacred enclosure. Similar descriptions are to be found in other apocalypses (e.g. Apoc. Baruch, 5; 2 Esd. 8.52). In Rabbinical literature the conception of paradise stands in contradistinction to hell. Paradise is occasionally referred to as "the world to come". Occurs in the New Testament only in Luke 23:43; 2 Cor. 12:4 and Rev. 2:7.

[33] *Blastano*, sprout, develop growth (of vegetation). Occurs 4 times in the New Testament: also in Mark 4:27; Heb. 9:4; James 5:18. See *P.Haun*, 2.23.9 (Egypt, III) letter, "The new planting has sprouted with the suckers, as it is harvest time"; IG *XIV* 607e.1, 4 (Karalis in Sardinia, 1 BC-1 CE), epitaph, "Pomptilla, may your bones sprout into violets and lilies, and may you bloom among the rose petals and the sweetly smelling crocus and the everlasting amaranth, and may you sprout into the lovely flowers of the snowdrop."

[34] Lit: "fine", "favorable", "good", but here is a positive used as a comparative with *mallon* (v. 42). The use of the positive of the adjective for the comparative is Semitic, although there are infrequent Classical parallels.

[35] Gehenna represented the rubbish dump outside Jerusalem. It was used for burning the bodies of the worst criminals. It was full of maggots and smoke. It was literally the Valley of Hinnon, *Ge Hinnom* in Hebrew.

[36] Verse 44 was added by copyists.

[37] The rest of verse 45 and all of verse 46 were added by copyists.

[38] Is. 66:24.

[39] The Greek version may be P.Oxy. 655d.1-5 as it is very fragmentary.

[40] Word for word "The body's light is the eye" but is in fact an idiom. "Eye" was the Greek metaphor for generosity. Here *ophthalmos*, but note, *omma*, "eye" is a formally polite term of endearment meaning "treasure", cf. Aristophanes, *Acharnians*, 1184; Aeschylus, *Cho*. 238; Sophocles, *Aj*. 977.

[41] *Poneros*, eye being evil, is Greek idiom for being greedy and stingy.

[42] *Poneros*: eye being evil is Greek idiom for being stingy or greedy.

[43] *Philostorgos*, regard, affection, occurs only here in New Testament. MM provide no documentary examples, although *IG*, *IGRR*, and *OGIS* were available in their time. Appears in *P.Oxy* 11.1380 (cf. *I.Kyme* 41) where Isis sees it as her role to promote *philostoria*, in families. See also *P.Tebt*. 2.408.5-10 (3 CE); *P.Oxy*. 495; *P.Grenf*. 2.71. To date no examples of the adjective have been found in the papyri. For the adjective, see also *P.Flor*. 3.338.10-12 (Arsinoite nome, III) where *philostorgos* forms a hendiadys with *spoude*.

[44] *Philadelphia*, love for fellow believers, love for fellow members of an association, love for siblings. This is the more common word for love of fellow believers in the New Testament. The cognate term *philadelphos* occurs only in 1 Peter 3:8 in the N.T. *Philadelphia*, and *philadelphos*, occur on Jewish inscriptions, for example, *CIJ* 1.125, 321, 263; *CIJ* 2.815, 1488, 1489. The

cognate term *philadelphos* occurs, for example, in *SEG* 1157, "Here lies Philippus, lover of his fellow believers, who lived thirty-three years." See also *SEG* 1511. *Philadelphos* also occurs in *CIJ* 2.1516, an epitaph for the 16 y.o. unmarried girl Sabbathin, *mikra philadephe*. The word is found on an epitaph for a woman, *SEG* 20.534, and on an epitaph for a man, *SEG* 20.524.

[45] See, for example, *P.Iand.* 6, a letter to "fellow believers", and *CE* 13, a letter from John the Deacon to a "fellow believer". Moulton and Milligan (MM), the lexicon of the papyri discovered prior to the early 1900s, state, "For the use of *adelphoi* to denote members of the same religious community cf. *P.Tor* 1 i.20 (ii BC)…and in *P.Par* 42 I etc (ii BC) the same designation is applied to the 'fellows' of a religious corporation established in the Serapeum of Memphis." They also cite *P.Tebt* 1.12 on which one town clerk addresses another as *adelphos*. For *adelphos* as a term of address (to people who are not siblings), they cite *P.Flor* II.228 (3 CE); *P.Tebt* II.314.12 (2 CE); *BGU* IV. 1209.2 (23 BC). For its use as "fellow believer" in the Christian papyri they cite *P.Grenf* II.73.

[46] To change one's mind or reverse one's attitude. "Repent" is a coined religious term.

[47] The Greek version is very fragmentary. P.Oxy 1.22.

[48] *Pantos* used in strong affirmations.

[49] *Iatros*, a qualified medical practitioner, *I.Stratonikeia* 2.1.1202.6, 11 (Stratonikeia, II) "Epaphroditos, you raised up many sick people. As a doctor you were very friendly to everyone, and good at your profession and diligent in character, for you learnt deeper understanding of your profession. But you could not save yourself from disease, for Fate is more masterful than doctors"; *P.Oxy* 1.40.5, 9 (Oxyrhynchos, II-III), "Psasnis presented himself and said, 'I am a doctor by profession and have treated these very people who have brought the case against me.' Eudaimon said, 'Perhaps you treated them badly. Inform the *strategos* if you are a public service doctor, suitably qualified, for then you will have immunity from the case"; *IG* II^2, 3.2.6873.4 (Akharnai, IV), "Here lies Phanostrate, midwife and doctor, who caused pain to no one, and who all missed when she died"; *IG* II^2, 3.2.9719.2 (Athens, 1), "Kallias the son [of N], of Miletos, doctor", *I.Eph* 6.2304.6 (Ephesos, 1-11), "The council takes care of the sarcophagus of the

doctors of the Mouseion in Ephesos", *P.Oxy* 1.51.4 (Oxyrhynchos, 173), "To Claudianus the *strategos* from Dionysos son of Apollodoros son of Dionysos of the city of Oxyrhynchos, public doctor. Today I was requested by you, through your assistant Herakleides, to inspect the corpse of a person found hanged, Hierax, and to report to you the situation as I ascertained it to be"; *P.Cair.Zen* 4.59571.9 (Philadelphia, 242 BC), "Please buy the cushions and carpets for Neon the doctor, so he can have them when he arrives. He was just now complaining about them. Bear in mind that Neon is a success with the king"; *P.Oxy* 42.3078.3 (Oxyrhynchos, II), "If you allow me to use Hermonios of Hermapolis, doctor, to treat my eyes…"

[50] *Therapeuo* describes the result of treatment which embraces physical and psychological therapies, and usually involves a permanent change of lifestyle. (IG IV^2 1, no. 126.) Continuity of action is always stressed with this verb. *L. Wells, The Greek language of Healing from Homer to New Testament Times, (Berlin: Walter de Gruyter, 1998)*, pp. 35, 39, 83, 510. In Thucydides' graphic account of the plague, either the present participle is used (2.47.4; 2.51.2; 2.51.3), or the cognate form (2.51.4) or the future participle (2.51.5). Xenophon's use of the word (*Cyropaedia* 3.2.12; *Memorabilia* 4.3.9) echoes that of Thucydides. From Isocrates' writing, it is evident that the concept of emotional support is implicit. Isocrates, *Aegineticus* 11, 20-33 describes treatment, and the resultant healing demands a response in the person who needs the healing – this person takes an active part in the healing process. Note that the opposite Greek word means "neglect". *Therapeuo,* is associated with hearing the Word and is often associated with a preaching context. It is ongoing: recovery may be rapid or slow.

Diogenes Laertes says the terms that Epicurus used for things were "ordinary" terms. *DL* 10.13. Where Epicurus uses the verb *therapeuo* to mean heal, the healing agent is the Word (*logos*) of the philosopher. Galen uses *therapeuo* to refer to the result of extended treatment, which reflects its use by Hippokratic authors. E.& L. Edelstein, *Asclepius: A Collection and interpretation of the testimonies*, 1945, Vol. 1., Baltimore, T 436, *Subfiguratio Empirica* Cp. X, p. 78; *IG* IV^2 1, no. 126. L. Wells, *op.cit.,* p. 88 states, "Thus Galen is consistent in his use of *therapeuo* to describe medical treatment, usually of an extended nature, that should be successful (but may not be successful in some circumstances)." Galen sees the need for *therapeuo* to treat "failures of function". *Galen: On the natural faculties*, (trans. A.J. Brock) (London: The Loeb Classical Library of Galen, 1979), *De naturalibus facultatibus*, 2.9 [2.126K.] pp. 194-196. The use of *therapeuo* by the Hippokratic medical school indicates that recovery may be slow or rapid. *Regimen* III.75.

Aristides (Publius Aelius) was famous for his precision of style, and for this reason his use of Greek healing language is instructive. He uses the term *therapeuo* as "medical treatment". Significantly, he uses the opposite term for "neglect". Aristides, vol. 1, *trans*. C.A. Behr, (London: Loeb Classical Library Edition of *Aristides*, 1973), 1, 472, *Or.* 2.326, phrase repeated in 327. Philo uses the term *therapeuo* to include ridding oneself of griefs, fears, acts of greed, folly and injustice "and the countless host of other passions and vices". Philo, *The Contemplative Life*, (trans. F.H. Colson), (London: The Loeb Classical Library Edition of Philo, 1941), 2 Loeb 9, pp. 112-114. Philo makes it clear that *therapeuo* should be understood in a spiritual sense, and places *therapeuo* ideally in a teaching context. In Josephus, *therapeuo* refers to ongoing treatment which may or may not be successful. *Jewish Antiquities*, (*trans*. R. Marcus), (London: *The Loeb Classical Library of Josephus*, 1978), Vol. 6., 9-11, Ant., 9.121, p. 64. *therapeuo* is linked with teaching and preaching. It is a continuous process, and is linked with changing one's way of life. L. Wells states, "When passive it (*therapeuo*) describes the result of God's healing *logos*, but this result demands an active and ongoing response in the life of the hearer of the word. Thus humans can be both healed and themselves take an active part in the healing process." (*op.cit.*, p. 119); "*Therapeuo* is the visible effect of teaching and preaching, the 'action' product of the message." (*ibid.,* p. 152.)

In Greek literature from Homer to New Testament times, *therapeuo* usually occurs in the imperfect, suggesting ongoing action. It is rarely used in the aorist. *Therapeuo* is the most popular word in the New Testament language of healing. In fact, it appears almost twice as often as the other New Testament popular word for healing, *iaomai*. This is totally contrary to the incidence of the verb in all Greek literature, as well as the Septuagint. In both the LXX and the New Testament it is the human word, whereas *iaomai* is the God word. The Greek speaker/listener understood all these concepts in the term *therapeuo* but there is no English equivalent.

[51] *Eipen de*. When these words occur between two utterances of Jesus, they indicate that there is an interval between what precedes and what follows. The report is condensed: another literary device of Luke's to avoid telling the whole account.

[52] *Deo*, "bind", "tie up", is a most significant word. The pagans used the same term in their magical practices. The word "bind" occurs in the magical spells (or more specifically, words of power) known as the *Ephesian Grammata*. For example, see magic spell against a competitor in a chariot race: "I conjure you up, holy beings and holy names; join in aiding this spell, and bind, enchant, thwart, strike, overturn etc..." See C.E. Arnold, *"Ephesians: Power and Magic: The Concept of Power in Ephesians in Light of Its Historical Setting,"* (New York: Baker Books, 1992), pp. 18, 33; A.F. Segal, "Hellenistic Magic: Some Questions of Definition," *Studies in Gnosticism and Hellenistic Religions* (Leiden: EPRO 91, 1981), 358.

[53] *Skeuoi*, furniture, movables, war equipment of any kind, implements of any kind, as opposed to fixtures.

[54] *Diarpazo* occurs only here in the New Testament. Used of "abduction" in J.W.B. Barns, *Studia Patristica* 1. *Papers Presented to the Second International Conference on Patristic Studies held at Christ Church*, Oxford, 1955. Part 1, edd. K. Aland/F.L. Cross (Texte und Untersuchungen 63; Berlin, 1957) 3-9; papyrus sheet, (Theadelphia, 6/4/343) *l*. 8, "settling upon my house and laying hands upon the wife (Nonna, mentioned above) of the said son of mine, he abducted her and removed her to his own house, though it was quite improper and quite illegal." Another compound of *harpazo*, *apharpazo*, occurs in *P.Sakaon* 48.20 of cattle stealing, and at *P.Sakaon* 36.15 of sheep stealing.

[55] *Ho oikos*, in Attic law, "the whole property", "the whole inheritance", cf. Hdt. 3.53

[56] Equally in the Greek, "Who can add to your lifespan?"

[57] Equally, "Which of you can add 1 cubit (18 inches/1 metre) to your height?"

[58] *Trugao*, to gather or pick, cf. *P.Oxy.* 3313, *ll.* 12, 13: "...we picked blooms which ought to have been picked tomorrow". See also Rev. 14:18, 19.

[59] *Kardias*, from the heart, which to the Greek meant the innermost part, the seat of emotions.

[60] Bible versions traditionally translate the personal pronoun here as "him", but the personal pronoun in the Greek is "it" following the neuter grammatical gender of "child". The gender of the child is not mentioned, and the Greek provides no clues.

[61] *Tapeinoo*: the noun refers to those who are of a low level in society – they may be poor, brought down in some way, weak, downcast.

[62] *Douleuo*, to be a slave servant, the noun being *doulos*. The word usually translated "servants" in most New Testament versions is not "servant", but "slave". It most certainly does not mean "bondservant", although some translators have used this as a euphemism for "slave". Slaves of the time were sometimes considered to be on the same level as children, and many were eventually adopted. Sometimes they inherited the master's property. Of course, others were treated as slaves in accordance with our modern perception of the word. Due to the complex nature of the relationship, the term is here rendered "slave servant". See discussion in S.R. Llewelyn, "Slaves and Masters" *NDIEC* 6.48-81; "The Legal Capacity of a Slave", *NDIEC* 7.165f.

[63] *Mamonas*. Mammon was a common Hebrew word in the second temple period. It appears in Ben Sira (Ecclesiastes) 31:11 and in the Mishnaic Hebrew of first century Jewish teachers. Contemporary Jewish commentary interpreted the word as "wealth", as did the Qumran writings. Some commentaries wrongly state that it is an Aramaic word exclusively or that Mammon was the Syrian demon-god of greed or at the least the personification thereof. Such interpretations appear in *The Catholic Encyclopedia*, Vol IX, New York 1910; C. Padjen, "Mammon", Dept. Theology, University of Notre Dame, 1997; A.L. Munroe, "Money, Mammon and Wealth", Paper presented at the Faith-Learning Institute, Cedarville College, (Cedarville, OH, 1995).

[64] Mark makes the distinction between *neos*, "new" (of time), and *kainos*, "fresh" (of quality).

[65] Verse 21 (omitted here) is not original and was added by copyists.

[66] *Artheti* is the aorist imperative passive of *airo*, "be seized", "be snatched up", not "be removed". "Remove" in the sense "transfer" or "take away" is *aphaireo*, which occurs in Mark 14:47. The translation "remove" usually occurs in the active sense. A common Greek word for "remove" in the sense "carry away" is *apophero* which occurs in Mark 15:1. In the Greek the actual words used for the mountain are "be snatched up" not "be removed". Snatching up or seizing is a decisive action: "removing" does not have the same connotations.

[67] *Diakrinomai*, the middle voice, to decide, not "doubt" or "hesitate". It also occurs in James 1:6. Often mistranslated "doubt" or "hesitate", but "doubt" is *apisteo* which occurs, for example, in Mark 16:11, 16. To hesitate or doubt (be perplexed) is *aporeo*, cf. Mark 6:20.

[68] *Ptokhos*, "financially destitute", not merely *penikhros*, "poor". The widow in Luke 21:3 was described as *penikhros*, "poor", before she had put all her funds into the offering box and *ptokhos*, afterwards. *Penikhros* occurs in *P.Oxy.* 3273 and tells of the confusion between two men of the same name and same village. One was mistakenly nominated for the other man's office, although he was *athetos kai penikhros*, lacking the financial means to be appointed to the office. *Ptokhos*, is the word used for beggars.

[69] *Miseo*, "hate" is not always as strong as, and has a wider meaning than, the English word "hate". For example, Homer uses it in the sense "Zeus hated (did not allow) that he should become a prey to the enemy dogs of Troy", *Iliad* 17.272, and Aristophanes uses it in the sense "passion", "grudging" cf. *Birds* 36.

[70] *Blastano*, sprout, develop growth (of vegetation). Occurs 4 times in the New Testament: also in Mark 4:27; Heb. 9:4; James 5:18. See *P.Haun*, 2.23.9 (Egypt, III) letter, "The new planting has sprouted with the suckers, as it is harvest time"; IG *XIV* 607e.1, 4 (Karalis in Sardinia, 1 BC-1 CE), epitaph, "Pomptilla, may your bones sprout into violets and lilies, and may you bloom among the rose petals and the sweetly smelling crocus and the everlasting amaranth, and may you sprout into the lovely flowers of the snowdrop."

[71] *Teknion*, a diminutive of *teknon*, a term of endearment and not of immaturity. "Member" or "child".

[72] The word "openly" does not appear here, nor is there any implication of it in the grammar. It appears in the Textus Receptus, and thereby in the KJV, as it was added by copyists in order to make a parallelism with the preceding phrase "in secret".

[73] *Blepontes, akouontes*, participles with concessive force.

[74] Isaiah 6:9.

[75] *Me eis theon plouton.* Either "by God's way", "in God's way". The use of *eis* may be the local use ("by entering God's way"), the metaphorical use (less likely, "for God"), or the use equivalent to a pure dative, ("in God's way", "by God's way") particularly as Luke commonly does not maintain the difference between *eis* and *en*, and there are plentiful instances in the New Testament of *eis*, with accusative being used for the simple dative.

[76] The sending of the messenger was according to Jewish custom.

[77] *Paraiteomai*, "decline", "refuse", "decline an invitation", "excuse oneself from" cf. Polyb. 5.27. An inscription records that a man by the name of Tiberius Claudius Marcianus was the victor in a wrestling match, as his opponents declined (threw in the towel) when they saw him stripped for the match. *CMRDM* (Pisidian Antioch, post 293) 1.164. 14-18.

[78] The fence was protection from wild animals.

[79] The tower had two purposes, as a watchtower and also as a shelter for the farmers.

[80] Again, needs to be translated by a colloquial expression.

[81] Meaning of *kephalioo* unknown in this context and elsewhere in Greek means "to sum up". Although the verb has something to do with "head", "wig", "source", "conclusion", there is no verb with the meaning "to wound in the head" in extant Greek literature. See discussion in Taylor, *op.cit.*, p. 474; *NDIEC* 3.70; 4.107.

[82] Psalm 118:22, 23.

[83] Psalm 118:22. There is no mention of "chief" in this scripture. The word "chief" is based on a mistranslation of *kephale*, "source".

[84] *Aphorizo*, to mark off by boundaries, to banish.

[85] Luke 10:2 is almost word-for-word with the quote of Matt. 9:37-38, except Luke reverses Matthew's order of the words "throw out" and "workers" placing less emphasis on the word "throw out."

[86] *Parthenos*. See note on Matt. 1:23.

[87] The evidence for and against the inclusion of the words *tou numphiou*, "and the bride", is not conclusive. Metzger, *op.cit.,* p. 52.

[88] *Pros* with accusative in its meaning "stayed with".

[89] Aorist tense referring to a point-of-time event, rather than to a continual event.

[90] *Ho huios tou anthropou*, meaning a person associated with humanity, a translation of *bar nasha*, an Aramaic periphrasis for "person", would be read word for word as "one associated with humanity" (as it is in non-gender specific language and "humanity" is in the singular). However, *bar nasha* means "one associated with people", "a person", "the person", "humanity", "the representative person". *The Anchor Bible* translates "The Man". The title is a direct reference to Daniel 7:13-14. See lengthy discussion in J. Massingberd Ford, "'Son of Man – A Euphemism?" *JBL* 87 (1968), 257-67: Albright, W.F. and Mann, C.S. *Matthew: A New Translation with Introduction and Commentary*, (New York: Doubleday, 1982), pp. CLVI-CLVII, 95; G. Dalman, *The Works of Jesus*, Eng. trans. by D.M. Kay, (Edinburgh, 1902); V. Taylor, *op.cit.*, p. 197.

Huios with a noun refers to a member of a class of people, and should not be translated as "son/child of". The *Benai Israel*, translated in the KJV as "children/sons of Israel" should be translated as "members of the class of people called Israel" = "Israelites". The expression is also Greek, and found as early as Homer.

Note also that *anthropos* is the word for human, humanity, person. Grammatically, it is the common gender and not the masculine.

[91] Jesus is traveling. He is not saying he is a homeless person, merely that he is not in his home town and has nowhere to stay the night.

[92] Jesus certainly was not poor and homeless. He was traveling at the time and was merely stating that he had nowhere to stay for the night.

[93] As "ask", "search" and "knock" are present imperatives, there has been much written that the sense is iterative and must be translated "keep on asking", "keep on searching", "keep on knocking". While this can be correct, it is also correct to state that the

present imperative was used in general precepts (whether or not to an individual) concerning attitudes and conduct, and the aorist was preferred in commands related to conduct for specific cases. R.W. Funk in his revision of Blass and Debrunner's *A Greek Grammar of the New Testament and Other Early Christian Literature*, (Chicago: C.U.P., 1961), notes that the aorist imperative was much less frequent than the present imperative in the New Testament, for the above context. He notes that the same thing holds true for the Cretan inscriptions, p. 172.

[94] *Anaperos*, "crippled" ("physically defective or mutilated"), occurs only here and in verse 21 in the New Testament, and is a rare word. See *P.Coll.Youtie* 1.16.5, 30 (Oxyrhynchos, 109 BC), a petition from a disabled soldier, "To Ptolemais, kinsman and strategos, from Petermouthis son of Peteesis,...among those recruited by Khmomenis, being a crippled tailor as well, ...and living in Oxyrhynchos in the same district...despising me as being helpless and a cripple..."

[95] *Adelphoi*. See note on Matt. 5:22. Here Jesus uses the collective term for siblings, and then to be emphatic follows with the separate terms.

[96] The KJV deliberately reverses the order of "mother and brothers", putting "brothers" first. Tyndale's 1534 translation correctly puts "mothers" first.

[97] *Agreuo*, "to hook" or "to catch out", a Greek term used in fishing.

[98] The poll-tax was paid directly into the Imperial *fiscus* and was especially hated by the Jews as a sign of subjection, and also because the coin bore the image and inscription of Caesar. The question was carefully posed to Jesus: an affirmative would disgust the people (Jews), and a negative reply would set the Roman authorities against him. Note that Jesus' reply was ambiguous. Daube states, "(This) is by no means a counsel of subservience to the state, rather one of minimum performance." D. Daube, "Responsibilities of Masters and Disciples in the Gospels", *NTS* 19 (1972/3) 15.

[99] *hupokrisis*, behaviour of a *hupokrites*. See note 95.

[100] *Apodidomi*, "give back". The verb implies either that the poll-tax is a debt, or that Caesar should get what's coming to him.

[101] A denarius.

[102] *Artheti* is the aorist imperative passive of *airo*, "be seized", "be snatched up", not "be removed". "Remove" in the sense "transfer" or "take away" is *aphaireo*, which occurs in Mark 14:47. The translation "remove" usually occurs in the active sense. A common Greek word for "remove" in the sense "carry away" is *apophero* which occurs in Mark 15:1. In the Greek the actual words used for the mountain are "be snatched up" not "be removed". Snatching up or seizing is a decisive action: "removing" does not have the same connotations.

[103] *Diakrinomai*, the middle voice, to decide, not "doubt" or "hesitate". It also occurs in James 1:6. Often mistranslated "doubt" or "hesitate", but "doubt" is *apisteo* which occurs, for example, in Mark 16:11, 16. To hesitate or doubt (be perplexed) is *aporeo*, cf. Mark 6:20.

[104] *Planao* "to wander off the path", the cognate noun being, *plane*. See Rom. 1:27. *Planao* occurs twice in this verse, and once in the next, and elsewhere in Matt. in 22:29; 24:4, 5, 11, 24.

Dr A. Nyland is also the translator of

The Book of Jubilees

This is a new (2011) easy-to-read translation and not one of the many century-old public domain translations. The Book of Jubilees contains information additional to Genesis and early Exodus, and is the account from creation to the early times of Moses. The Book of Jubilees claims to be told to Moses by angels when he was on Mount Sinai. One of the Dead Sea Scrolls, The Damascus Document, states that the Book of Jubilees reveals divine secrets "to which Israel has turned a blind eye." The Essenes, a Jewish sect who lived from the 2nd c. BCE to the 1st c. ACE, coveted the Book of Jubilees and kept it in their library. Jubilees are seven "year-weeks," a year-week being a period of seven years, so a jubilee is 49 years.

The Source New Testament with Extensive Notes on Greek Word Meaning

The Source New Testament with Extensive Notes on Greek Word Meaning contains abundant and detailed documentation for the meaning of hundreds of Greek words which appear in the New Testament. The Source is the only New Testament translation based on word meaning evidence from the recently discovered papyri and inscriptions. For centuries, translators had to guess the meaning of hundreds of New Testament words. After 1976, huge numbers of papyri and inscriptions were discovered containing these words in everyday documentation thus revealing their meaning. *The Source* is the only New Testament translation by a Classical Greek scholar (rather than theologian) and not financed or translated by a committee of a specific denomination.

Book of Enoch: Angels, Watchers and Nephilim

The Book of Enoch contains accounts of the Watchers, a class of angel, who came to earth, taught humans weapons, alchemy, spell potions, sorcery, astrology, and astronomy. The Watchers also married human women and produced the Nephilim. For this, they were punished and cast into Tartarus. This is also mentioned in the New Testament. This is an easy to read translation of The Book of Enoch with additional information on angels, Watchers, and Nephilim.

Second Book of Enoch (2 Enoch, Secrets of Enoch, Slavonic Enoch)

The Second Book of Enoch was originally written in Greek at Alexandria although some parts of the text were written in Hebrew in Palestine. It is dated to the 1st century prior to the destruction of the Temple in 70 CE. Two angels take Enoch into six heavens. Enoch is then taken by Gabriel into the seventh heaven and then by Michael into the Lord's presence. This book contains the extended version of 2 Enoch, The Exaltation of Melchizedek, and is an easy to read translation, with notes and cross references to both scripture and contemporary writings.

Third Book of Enoch (3 Enoch, Merkabah Hebrew Book of Enoch)

3 Enoch is also known as The Hebrew Book of Enoch, as the evidence suggests it was originally written in Hebrew. 3 Enoch is also known as Sefer Hekhalot, meaning Book of Palaces. In 3 Enoch, Enoch ascends to heaven and is transformed into the angel Metatron. The Talmud does not state this, but the tradition is found in the earliest Kabbalists. Jewish mysticism traces to the Merkabah practices of the 1st c. CE. The goal of Merkabah Mysticism was to enter a trance-like state by means of fasting, meditation, prayer and incantation, and thus ascend to God's heavenly throne room and experience God's Throne-Chariot (Hebrew: "Merkabah").

Complete Books of Enoch: 1 Enoch (First Book of Enoch), 2 Enoch (Secrets of Enoch), 3 Enoch (Hebrew Book of Enoch)

1 Enoch tells of the Watchers, a class of angel, who taught humans weapons, spell potions, root cuttings, astrology, astronomy, and alchemies. The Watchers also slept with human women and produced the Nephilim. For this, they were imprisoned and cast into Tartarus. This is also mentioned in the New Testament. In 2 Enoch, two angels take Enoch through the 7 heavens. This contains the extended version of 2 Enoch, The Exaltation of Melchizedek. In 3 Enoch, Enoch ascends to heaven and is transformed into the angel Metatron. This is about the Merkabah and is of interest to Kabbalists.

Dr A. Nyland is also the author of (for example):

Angels, Archangels and Angel Categories: What the Ancients Said

Are you tired of reading conflicting reports about angels? Do you read about angels only to discover that the author relied on fiction works and not ancient sources? In this easy to read book, Dr Nyland looks at actual ancient sources about angels, archangels, and angel categories such as cherubim, seraphim, the Watchers, the "sons of God," and the Nephilim. If you want to get the facts about angels, this book is for you.

Fallen Angels, Watchers, Giants, Nephilim and Evil

This is an easy-to-read book suited to anyone with an interest in the subject, but has full scholarly notes to primary sources. Watchers were a class of angel who came to earth and taught weapons, spell potions, root cuttings, astrology, astronomy and alchemies to the humans living on earth. Some of the Watchers slept with human women. For this they were thrown into Tartarus. Nephilim were the progeny of the Watchers and the human women. Greek mythology speaks of *gigantes* being thrown into Tartarus. *Gigantes* is the word which the Septuagint (the ancient Greek translation of the Hebrew Bible dated to the 3rd to 2nd centuries BCE) uses to translate the Hebrew word "Nephilim," and is translated into English as "Giants."

Idioms such as the mistranslation "sons of God," which have rightly confused those who have no knowledge of ancient languages, are explained fully. The book avoids theological pontificating and ramblings, and adheres instead to actual evidence.

among other books

About the Author

Dr A. Nyland is an ancient language scholar and historian who served as faculty at the University of New England, Australia. Dr Nyland is also the translator of "The Complete Books of Enoch,"

"The Source New Testament with Extensive Notes on Greek Word Meaning," the ancient Hittite "Kikkuli Text," and "The Psalms: Translation with Notes" and the author of "A Devil of a Job to Find Satan in the Bible."

3486509R00049

Printed in Great Britain
by Amazon.co.uk, Ltd.,
Marston Gate.